SANTA FE STYLE

First published in the United States
of America in 1986 by
Rizzoli International Publications, Inc.
300 Park Avenue South
New York, NY 10010

Library of Congress Cataloging-in-Publication Data

Mather, Christine.
  Santa Fe style

  1. Architecture, Domestic—New
Mexico—Santa Fe. 2. Pueblos—New
Mexico—Influence. 3. Vernacular
architecture—New Mexico—Santa Fe.
4. Interior decoration—New Mexico—
Santa Fe. 5. Indians of North America—
New Mexico—Civilization—Influence.
6. Hispanic Americans—New Mexico—
Civilization—Influence. 7. Santa Fe
(N.M.)—Buildings, structures, etc.
I. Woods, Sharon. II. Title.
NA7238.S364M3   1986   728'.09789'56   86–42715
ISBN 0–8478–0734–7 hardcover
ISBN 0–8478–2388–1 paperback

Set in type by Rainsford Type,
Ridgefield, Connecticut

Printed and bound in Japan
Distributed by St. Martin's Press
Reprinted in 1997, 1999
Reprinted in paperback 2001

SANTA FE STYLE

CHRISTINE MATHER
AND SHARON WOODS

DESIGN
BY PAUL HARDY

Photographs by Robert Reck,
Jack Parsons, and others

RIZZOLI
NEW YORK

CONTENTS

ACKNOWLEDGMENTS

Santa Fe has been our home for over a decade. Like many of its residents, we were attracted by its beauty, culture, and unique architecture. Christine's experience of New Mexico was greatly enriched by her work as curator of Spanish Colonial Art at the Museum of New Mexico and through contacts at Davis Mather Folk Art. Sharon has also worked with the architecture of northern New Mexico in her position as vice-president of Robert Woods Construction Company. We met as a result of an addition to the Mather home and quickly developed a dialogue based on our mutual interest in Santa Fe style. In our collaboration Christine has been the writer and Sharon the coordinator of photography, but our research and conversation often overlapped; we have both benefited from each other's experience.

Since the inception of the book we have had a great deal of support from others. We are especially grateful to our editor at Rizzoli, Lauren Shakely; to the designer, Paul Hardy, who immediately grasped the unique nature of Santa Fe; and to Jack Parsons and Robert Reck, and the other photographers who have so generously shared their vision and their resources with us.

We also thank those who let us into their homes and permitted us to disrupt their lives and privacy. We do not wish to further violate their privacy by thanking them by name, but we recognize their invaluable contribution to this book. Architects and designers Charles F. Johnson; Victor Johnson; Antoine Predock; Robert Peters; John Midyette; Betty Stewart, President, Stewart Construction Company, Inc., and Richard Yates have made Santa Fe a better place for all of us.

A number of others have extended their help in research, photography arrangements, and countless other resources. We thank particularly *Antiques* magazine, Irene Broome, John Cartwright, Ray Dewey, Linda Dressman at the Flower Market, Gayle Maxon, Gary Miller of the Lincoln County Trust, the Photograph Archive of the Museum of New Mexico, The Laura Gilpin Collection of the Amon Carter Museum of Art, Mark Nohl of *New Mexico Magazine*, Nathaniel Owings, Jr., Ford Ruthling, J. Paul Taylor, Burt Tauber, Christopher Webster, and the staff of the Bank of Santa Fe.

Finally, although we recognize that no author can succeed without the support of her family, we would like to thank ours, especially our husbands, Davis Mather and Robert Woods, not only for their respect and faith in us, but for their own personal experiences in Santa Fe, which have so enriched this book.

Christine Mather
and Sharon Woods
Santa Fe
April 1986

INTRODUCTION

The romantic aura of Santa Fe is hundreds of years old. The capital of the state of New Mexico, the city has fewer than 50,000 inhabitants, yet it was once the northernmost outpost of the Spanish Empire, the end of the trail for pioneer journeys during the Western expansion, and the crossroads between Latin and North America. What has imbued Santa Fe with its sense of romance and history is its remarkable ability to preserve a sense of identity in the face of pressures to conform. Santa Fe remains uniquely its own place, its residents stubbornly and stoically insisting that tradition take precedence over change.

When the Spanish first settled in Santa Fe in the early 1600s, life at this garrison was considered a great hardship, marked by perpetual shortage of necessities, absence of luxuries, and antagonism on the part of the native population. In fact it was in Santa Fe that the traditionally peaceful Pueblo Indians staged the only successful Indian rebellion against the Spanish Empire in North America, driving out the colonists for twelve years in the late seventeenth century. Slowly, America's other colonial history—the Spanish colonization of the West— evolved, and a new American lifestyle began to develop, a lifestyle steeped in Hispanic and Native American traditions and shaped by the exigencies and corresponding ingenuity of frontier life.

After Mexico gained independence from Spain in the revolt of 1821, the Santa Fe Trail was established linking the American East with the Southwest. When the first eastern Americans arrived in Santa Fe, they were surprised to find that this famed capital was not the metropolitan center they had expected, but rather a sleepy mer- cantile and governmental town, a true backwater of what once had been the mighty Spanish Empire. The newcomers reserved their most severe criticism for the long, low buildings of dirt with dirt floors that made up the town of Santa Fe—Puritan America encountered Latin America, and the result was a period of confusion and rivalry. The Eastern Americans were less offended by the Native Americans, whose exotic ways they considered quaint. Although New Mexico became United States territory in 1846, it was nearly a full century before East truly met West in Santa Fe, and the "newcomers" became seasoned enough to appreciate the richness of their new culture.

Below: Western farming was a hard day's work for the entire family at the turn of the century. Right: Spring over Rancho de Taos to the north of Santa Fe shows the adobe settlement with its backdrop of mountains.

New Mexico's first permanent residents, the Native Americans whose ancestors first inhabited the region hundreds of years before Europeans arrived, have been primary contributors to the enduring style of the land and its people. Over the centuries Pueblo Indians created modest, functional communities that provided protection from the elements and security from hostile outsiders. Their buildings are characterized by blocks of multistoried dwellings built around a central plaza. Puddled adobe or ashlar masonry, log roofs, and dirt flooring were the modest materials used to fashion sophisticated structures. Perhaps it is the simplicity of these dwellings that has most determined the plain, integrated human setting of Santa Fe and its environs. Here man and landscape come together with such mutual benefit that the landscape is brought into human scale, and human inhabitation makes no attempt to master elements beyond its scope.

While Native Americans had a strong and far-reaching impact on the land and man's relationship to it, the Spanish colonists developed a true regional style. Building types in Santa Fe all have clear Spanish peninsular antecedents. The materials and environment of the New World created a mixture of style elements now recognizable as characteristically New Mexican. The casual plainness of the architecture, the contrasts between light and dark, the massive solidity of walls, doors, and ceiling beams, the spareness or absence of decoration, the integrity of materials, and the interwoven harmony of all of these elements have engendered a style that is unmistakably Santa Fe. Few details of daily living in the American Southwest have escaped Spanish influence. Buildings, town plans, street patterns, ranch practices, water usage, religion, politics, place names, cuisine, plant life, and music—all bear the stamp of the Spanish culture.

At the end of the Trail, at the terminus of the Camino Real, the Santa Fe Plaza is the symbolic and literal crossroads of the American frontier and the Spanish Empire. It is the business center, the community gathering place, and the center of celebrations. The Plaza is a kind of family dinner table—a place to renew ties and resolve differences. Its central role in the lives of those who live in Santa Fe and in the arrangement of the community is part of the Spanish and Native American legacy.

Opposite page: "Bae-ie-schluch-a-ichin" (Slim, maker of silver) reads the old inscription on this photograph made of a Navajo jeweler in 1885. The concho belt he displays in his lap is a type still being made by the Navajos today. Below: Palace of the Governors, an important Santa Fe landmark on the Plaza, as it looked in 1881.

Bordering the Plaza's northern edge is another symbol of Santa Fe life—the Palace of the Governors, the oldest public building in the United States. Its long single-story facade is always in the midst of renovation and renewal; it is an adobe monument to endurance. Until relatively recent times it also served as the home of the New Mexican governors, typifying the domestic design of Hispanic tradition.

With the opening of the Santa Fe Trail, home design was further modified by the arrival of new goods from the East—industrially manufactured glass and metal, along with the expertise to mill lumber and the decorative ideas of Victorian America. The territorial style replaced the simple pueblo adobe style by adaptation rather than substitution. The presence of the United States army gave a sense of security that permitted the fortress construction of the hacienda to relax into a more open ranch. In town, as life became easier, decoration became more elaborate. Santa Fe residents eagerly adopted the whimsical volutes and scrolls of Victorian gingerbread, combining them—with surprising success—with the heavy walls of the Spanish dwelling style. By the early twentieth century, the adaptability of Santa Fe threatened the survival of its individual style by homogenization. Santa Fe's first resident artist, Carlos Vierra, spearheaded the revival of old styles by building a home in 1918 based on a combination of regional architecture and modifications essential for contemporary living. His perception of New Mexico's adobe homes as works of art became a community's sense of pride. Vierra correctly assessed what the preservation of Santa Fe would mean to its future:

"Progress in Santa Fe is not so likely to come through imitation of methods and customs of any other town as through an appreciation and development of the great advantages we have had from the beginning."

However Santa Fe changes, it remains the same. Today's architecture, modified to Santa Fe's building codes, has only amplified the tradition with ideas that suit the environment and lifestyle of the region. Passive-solar architecture, once thought to be an engineering impossibility, has become commonplace in the sunny Santa Fe climate, and the dramatic geometric facades perched on mesas in the hills around Santa Fe complement the landscape as well as take utmost advantage of its benefits. As Santa Fe's stylistic influence is felt in other parts of the country, its adherence to tradition and well-considered response to change are ever more appreciated.

Santa Fe resident Professor Wood and his family pose in front of their home in 1912.

SANTA FE SETTING

The American frontier may no longer exist, but Santa Fe is still a town in awe of its surroundings. The rugged Sangre de Cristo mountains, the gentle pinyon-dotted foothills, and the vast blue sky are a background that no design of man can improve.

Above: Pink cactus flower. Right: Anasazi cave dwellings in Canyon de Chelly, Arizona, a favorite subject of photographers since the 1860s.

For nearly two hundred million years the contours of the New Mexican landscape have remained much the same. The first Indians of ten thousand years ago, the Spanish settlers of the seventeenth century, the U.S. Geological survey expeditions of the nineteenth century, and present-day visitors have all been witness to an awe-inspiring terrain. Whether the sandstone cliffs of Canyon de Chelly in the northeast or the Sangre de Cristos near Santa Fe, this backdrop of spectacular natural beauty has influenced dwelling styles from Neolithic to modern times.

The origins of the region's geology are in the Cenozoic era, when the great rock formations were created, and in the Jurassic age, when they were raised from the earth's crust as the tail end of the Rocky Mountain chain. The monumental slanting slabs of rock, with their great power and antiquity, have both a comforting and a threatening presence. The pale yellow to ruddy tones of the sandstone cast their warm hues over the landscape and color the walls of adobe structures.

Other colors change with the seasons: lilacs frame doorways and hang over rail fences in springtime; pink hollyhocks grace a white-painted *portal* in summer. In the fall,

aspens change quickly, fringing hillsides with golden yellow. Green and red chilies, and strings of blue corn, hang to dry beside mounds of yellow and orange melons. Even winter is more than the white-on-white combination of snow and painted adobe; it is a subtle range of pastel blues and forest greens, tinted rose by the evening sun.

Santa Fe builders have tampered very little with the wonder of this setting. The shelters they have constructed, whether the Pre-Columbian cave dwellings of the Anasazi or the adobe homes of Santa Fe today, relate to their surroundings so intimately that they seem to be a part of nature's design.

Above Kitchen Mesa at Ghost Ranch near Abiquiu, New Mexico, a rainbow emerges after a thunderstorm.

LIGHT

The light in Santa Fe has special purity and clarity. Strong contrasts of light and dark throw every element of the environment into sharp relief: each needle of the pine tree stands out distinctly; the shadows beside a building outline it with stark precision. Whether it is the altitude, the dry crisp air, the barren geometry of the landscape, or all of these elements, the rare quality of light in Santa Fe has seduced visitors and inspired artists.

Even the dying light has its attractions. Shadows grow longer and more dramatic, as the sunset burnishes adobe and wood with gold.

Corbels and beams, parapet walls, and the setting sun upon them at the Amelia Hollenbeck home in Santa Fe.

NATIVE MATERIALS

Until the railroad reached Santa Fe in the late nineteenth century, inhabitants built with whatever materials were at hand. Beginning in about A.D. 100, when the early Indians known collectively as the Anasazi permanently settled in the region, these materials consisted primarily of the mud, sand, and clay mixture called adobe, along with pine logs and stone. The distinctive Pre-Columbian structures built into cliffs—still seen in such architectural sites as Canyon de Chelly—left their mark on local building styles, even after the arrival of Europeans. The Spanish colonists developed adobe into bricks in imitation of the stone blocks they had known in Spain and used them to build haciendas and village churches. The basic building blocks of Southwestern architecture are still much the same. Cement frequently replaces adobe in modern structures, but the colors and designs echo the traditional forms.

Left: Built to imitate the communal dwellings of Indian Pueblos is a contemporary series of interrelated condominiums, Los Miradores, which mimics early architecture and building materials.

Left to right, top: Taos Pueblo home. Adobe wall at Fort Union, New Mexico. Front tower of the Saint Francis Auditorium of the Fine Arts Museum in Santa Fe. Second row: Top of Saint Francis in Santa Fe against a blue sky. Tiny window at Taos Pueblo. Ladder against a wall at the home of Carlos Vierra. Bottom row: Long, low adobe building in Santa Fe. Bank on Santa Fe's Plaza. Passageway at Taos Pueblo.

FENCES

The open spaces of the countryside have influenced the elements of Santa Fe style. Some features open the home to its surroundings; others protect it from them. Every building in the region that does not have an adobe wall seems to have a fence. The individual style of the home's owner is often proclaimed on these enclosures—whether it is a patriotic fervor, a sense of humor, or an appreciation of nature.

Cement and rock in a folk art fence in Mountainair, New Mexico, made by Pop Shaffer.

Left: Coyote fence made of cedar poles behind a wooden cart. Right: Patriotic picket fence in Villanueva, New Mexico.

WINDOWS

Santa Fe walls are simple, undulating, and monochromatic; windows are the playground of the imagination. Perhaps because the original adobe home was virtually windowless, today the window is a source of endless variety in color and design. Traditional windows include small rectangular openings with wooden shutters or vertical grills, and Greek Revival-style paned windows with plain wooden frames. Fancy molding with dentated, flaring, or scrolled embellishments became popular as Gothic revival taste arrived in the Southwest in the late nineteenth century. Dramatic picture windows are reserved for homes in the mountains, where they take advantage of panoramic views.

The territorial-style window at the left is a Santa Fe classic. At the right, the range of color and design in Santa Fe style, expressed in windows.

THE ROADSIDE WEST

Driving through the Southwest, the traveler passes through endless stretches of nearly featureless landscape only to be shaken from his stupor by bizarre roadside attractions. Homemade signs offer such comestibles as cactus candy and rattlesnake meat; and such treasures as fine "art" and meteorites. Ghost towns and movie sets alternate with inhabited settlements. The playfulness of contemporary Western charm is also a feature of indigenous design. Humorous and colorful touches leaven the historic solemnity of the true Southwest with the trappings of its popular legend.

In town a log cabin is spruced up with red and green paint, but its ranch character remains intact.

Along the highways a giant steer reminds the traveler to Eat More Beef.

Eaves Ranch outside of Santa Fe is the quintessential Western town, a fantasy built for one of the many cowboy movies filmed beneath the clear Santa Fe skies.

SPANISH MISSIONS

The northward movement of the Spanish brought not only settlements and garrisons to the territory along the Rio Grande, but also missions. With the help of Indian builders, the Franciscan friars who followed Juan de Oñate to New Mexico in the seventeenth century soon erected adobe churches. These massive structures are now not only the most recognizable architectural monuments of the Southwest; they are also among the oldest extant buildings of the colonial period in the United States.

Crosses can be found not only on every church tower and decorated with flowers in the village cemetery, but also along the roadside marking the passing of a soul.

28

Adobe churches often have a peaked roof, sometimes with a stepped gable, which is always topped with a cross. A simple hole in the whitewashed adobe wall holds the church bell, which would have been one of the most precious possessions of the mission. Adobe churches are still in use today, although smaller churches and private chapels frequently lie abandoned, their white walls and crosses still prominent against blue sky.

Left: The facade of the Church of San Geronimo at Taos Pueblo. Above: Perched on an eroded tower at San Jose de Gracia, Trampas, is a small cupola.

LADDERS

Ladders are seen all over New Mexico, but their true home is in the Indian pueblo. Until well into the nineteenth century, the multilevel pueblo homes had no doorways, but were entered by openings in the roof. At night the ladders that gave access to the first level were pulled up to protect the pueblo from intruders.

The ladders that connected different stories of the home played an important part in domestic arrangements. Enormous handsome ladders are also used to enter the kivas, the subterranean ceremonial rooms of the Pueblo Indians. The design of these ladders is functional and sturdy, and also suggests ceremonial significance.

Ladders at the Pueblos of Acoma and Taos are still a functional part of home life, much as they were in the dwellings of the Pueblo Indians' ancestors.

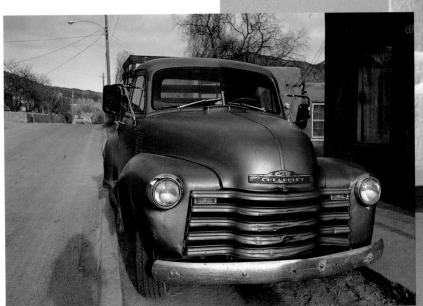

CARS

In the West, where long drives are commonplace, the car—especially the ubiquitous pickup truck—often becomes as important to the owner's sense of identity as his home. Cars and trucks often seem to match the houses outside of which they are parked, whether by design or by a serendipitous juxtaposition. Even the most dilapidated vehicle, reminder of a more romantic era of the automobile, can dress up the front of an adobe home.

AROUND SANTA FE

Spanish colonization of the Southwest has had a deep abiding impact on Santa Fe. Native Americans established a relationship to the land; the Spanish brought Western European ideas to blend with the Indian.

The unique Spanish, Indian, and Anglo-American heritage of Santa Fe has produced an eclectic visual treat. A thousand years of history and legend are summed up in the sights along streets and highways of New Mexico. Strings of corn and chilies, cowboys swinging lariats, the bright colors of the New Mexican flag (adapted from the symbol of the Zia Pueblo), and images of Spanish saints are all part of the look of the community. Although tourism has spawned myriad businesses and signs around the Plaza, Santa Fe has preserved the ambiance of a small southwestern town with legislation that determines the color, size, and design of facades and shop signs.

Left: *Portal* of Lujan House, Taos, New Mexico. **Right:** Glimpses of New Mexico present a mixture of elements from the diverse cultures of Native, Hispanic, and Anglo America.

Even the town plan of Santa Fe, a striking contrast to the grid plan of most Western towns and cities, grew according to regulations specified by the Spanish crown—with irregularities caused by Santa Fe's roots as a farming community. Long corridorlike streets tunnel through adobe one- and two-story buildings, then suddenly open out to reveal the Plaza, the literal and civic heart of town at the end of the Santa Fe Trail. Other primary streets follow the Santa Fe River or the agricultural ditches, *acequias*, which supported the farmers of early Santa Fe. Canyon Road runs parallel to the river. To the south, Acequia Madre (Mother Ditch) borders another major waterway. Many Santa Fe streets bear the names of their ultimate destinations: Galisteo, Agua Fria, Pecos, Old Taos Highway, and Cerrillos. Others have names that designate physical location: Water Street and Alto Street.

Right: Old wagon in front of Fenn Gallery, Santa Fe

PURE AND SIMPLE

Many Santa Fe homes, both old and newly built, are in the pueblo style. Like the Indian pueblos from which the style in part developed, these homes derive their charm from simple, functional materials; adobe bricks made from earth, sand, and water; carved or rough-hewn wood; and mud plaster in a range of warm hues.

Left: The colors of adobe plaster range from gray to yellow to brown, depending on where the clay and sand used in its manufacture are acquired. Above: a *santo*, or saint figure, made in New Mexico in the nineteenth century.

The earliest pueblo adobe houses were simple, consisting of a few rooms whose widths were determined by the length of the logs used as ceiling beams—usually about fifteen feet. Over these beams, called *vigas*, were laid *latillas* (cedar poles) and flat earthen roofs. *Canales*, the drainspouts that carry water through the parapet off the rooftop, were a crucial feature of pueblo-style construction. Poorly maintained or located *canales* could result in rapid destruction of the adobe walls, which were not only made of fragile sun-baked earth, but were plastered with similar material.

In early homes the walls were often very thick; it is not uncommon for an old home to have walls three to four feet deep. The few windows that pierced these monolithic facades were minute by today's standards. Their small size was determined not only by the unavailability of glass and iron and the need to keep out cold and heat, but also by the necessity for self-protection. Although the early colonists lived peacefully with Pueblo Indians, the Apache, the Comanche, and the Navajo often raided settled communities, both Spanish and Indian. The fortress-like appearance of the pueblo home reflects the

hardships of early New Mexican life.

In today's pueblo-style homes, modern convenience has modified but not diminished the style of Santa Fe's past. Outer windows are often small, in keeping with the pueblo tradition, while windows that look onto the inner courtyards (*placitas* in Spanish) or gardens are often of generous proportions. The elegant appearance of *vigas* and *latillas* are appreciated as a characteristic element of local design, and many homes incorporate original old ceiling beams, or reproductions of them, as a prominent feature of the home. Floors of natural materials—brick, flagstone, tile, or pine—replace the hard-packed earthen floors of the past, but preserve the early flavor of the style. When cement plaster is used instead of true adobe, it is colored and textured to match the original.

Santa Fe residents take pride in their Spanish and Indian heritage, and many of the region's finest homes take the pueblo style as their inspiration.

A weathered wooden door with an old iron knocker leads to a protected courtyard garden.

A PARED-DOWN HOME

The house built by the late Nathaniel Owings for himself and his wife, Margaret, is hardly the sort of structure one might expect from an architect of skyscrapers, but there is a similarity in the purity of the Owings home in Jacona, New Mexico, and the clean lines of modern architecture.

This house epitomizes the simple visual and mental life that New Mexico has to offer. Its materials are the time-honored building blocks of the pueblo home—adobe and wood. Inside, the house has an almost monastic serenity, achieved by emphasizing the integrity and plain beauty of the mud bricks and plaster, and allowing the ceilings of *vigas* and *latillas* to serve their purpose without unnecessary adornment. The monumental sculptural qualities of the materials provide the main reference point for the furnishings. Every object in the Owings home seems to have found its way into its surroundings by a gradual and unpretentious process by which every extraneous detail is eliminated, leaving only the essentials.

Below: When open, the large double gate frames the front of the house; when closed, it provides a sense of security. Right: At the front door an enormous nineteenth-century grain chest made in New Mexico.

Beneath the ancient cottonwoods that thrive in the valley in the area near Santa Fe called Jacona, the front porch, or *portal*, delicately embellished with turned spindles, shields the house from the direct southwestern sun. A small walled garden before the *portal* is planted with native and common plants that thrive in strong sunlight.

Double doors open onto a spare and serene—almost monastic—bedroom. Many of the furnishings of the Owings home are colonial Mexican or New Mexican in style. The heavy proportions and flat carving of this style derived from Old World taste of medieval times, which persisted into the nineteenth century in the New World. Leaded glass windows reinforce this sense of the past.

Looking across part of the large central room to the kitchen: a potbelly stove heats not only the kitchen but much of the rest of the home as well. Behind the stove the unplastered wall functions as a fire shield and also collects heat, reflecting it back into the room for a long time after the fire has died out. Adobe walls act in the same way, storing the heat of the day and releasing it at night as temperatures cool. Raised corner fireplaces, like the one at the far end of the kitchen, are efficient heating elements as well as distinctive features of Santa Fe style.

The large painted cupboard, *trastero*, at the left is topped by two Pueblo Indian pots. The rare New Mexican *santo* in the window, of carved and painted cottonwood, dates from the late eighteenth century. The cloth skirt of this figure of the Virgin was soaked in gesso and then attached to the wooden frame and painted. The technique of manufacture came from Spain, the source of many of the methods of construction and design motifs of the Southwest.

The woodwork elements at the right above are typical of the attention paid to detail in the Owings home: a territorial-style doorway, a saint figure, and a gatepost. Below, the pantheon of Hopi and Zuni spirits and gods is represented in kachinas. Although commonly called kachina "dolls," the figures are used as teaching aids in Pueblo religions, not as playthings. Like the religious dances and ceremonies held in the pueblos in the summertime, kachinas bring to life the spirit world of Native America.

A graceful territorial-style pediment and frame surround the doorway into Margaret Owing's small studio. Skylights between the ceiling beams provide natural light for the textile artist, one of whose weavings hangs on the studio wall.

The stylized cornstalks of the Navajo rug on the wall, the lustrous black Santa Clara Pueblo pottery, and the plain skin-and-rawhide Taos drums are characteristic of the bold arts of the Southwest, collected here in the studio of the late Nathaniel Owings.

ADOBE

Without adobe, New Mexican architecture would not exist. Used by Native Americans in prehistoric times, adobe was also known to the Spanish colonists in the seventeenth century. The word refers to the mixture of clay and sand, the bricks made from the mixture, and any home made of adobe. Early Indians used puddle adobe, a time-consuming process that required each successive layer to dry thoroughly before the next one was poured. Modern adobe structures are built from adobe bricks, a method introduced by the Spanish. Each brick, which weighs about twenty-five or thirty pounds, is formed in a simple mold; then the mold is removed and the brick is left to dry in the sun. An "adobe farm" is a vast field of brown squares bordered by stacks of adobe waiting for use. Before the advent of efficient transportation, adobes were almost always made on the site. The old adobe house almost literally grew up from the earth around it.

Many adobe buildings have more than a single course of brick; a double wall insures insulation and sound absorption, so the phrase "double adobe" has come to connote a desirable home. Large edifices, such as churches, sometimes had walls that were seven feet thick. Because each brick is formed by hand and is laid by hand, walls are irregular. Inside walls often bulge at the bottom, thin out at the top. A slightly crooked door frame, a curving *banco* for seating along the wall, an arched *nicho* for storage and display, corner fireplaces—all of these make the adobe house into a sculptural edifice that takes on a character of its own.

As it ages, adobe plaster takes on a characteristic surface of cracks and fissures that enhances the textural beauty of the material. The patterns on the side of this church at San Isidro, New Mexico, are as intricate as those of a contour map.

These adobes, drying in the sun at an "adobe farm," were ultimately used in the mosque built near Abiquiu, New Mexico.
Large buildings and complexes consist of many thousands of adobes. Although some parts of the Southwest have seen an increased use of "stabilized" adobe, which is treated with chemical additives to become moisture resistant, Santa Fe residents still prefer the original material. Because it lacks malleability, treated adobe does not have the plastic curves of true adobe.

True adobe plaster, once renewed annually by women plasterers called *enjarradoras*, is rarely used today. Instead of mud, sand, and straw, modern adobe walls are covered with stucco, but true adobe acquires an individual patina and texture as it ages. Santa Feans so appreciate this material that they often use it on interior walls or beneath protected *portales*, where wind and rain do not cause it to deteriorate.

Adobe buildings quickly erode if not properly maintained. Even the largest structures can almost disappear in a few years, leaving behind a mound of earth. Once the roof beams collapse, or an opening in a wall exposes the interior to the elements, the adobe house is doomed. Even modernization must be carefully planned, since pitched tin roofs and cement, when incorrectly applied, can cause the retention of moisture within walls, ultimately destroying the adobe inside.

HOUSE ON THE MESA

To the west of Santa Fe the high mesas that extend to the Rio Grande provide a dramatic plain from which all of the surrounding mountains can be seen. Houses built upon these mesas command a view that reaches to the Jemez Mountains on the west, the Sangre de Cristos toward the east, and the Sandia range to the south. The siting of this adobe home was chosen to take the utmost advantage of the breathtaking landscape. Since this was a second home for its owners, they had the luxury of being able to eliminate all of the usual clutter that often interferes with the original simplicity of a Santa Fe home's design.

The plain white walls are used as a foil for fine examples of local treasures—a Navajo rug in the style and color called Ganado red or a deer skull with antlers intact. *Bancos* and Taos-style daybeds are used for seating, often placed to face the large windows that frame extraordinary vistas. In the summer, the life of the house is directed to the outdoors, in a vast patio with excellent views from every side.

The great sculptural properties of adobe create walls that flow organically into projections and recesses that function as furniture while giving a sense of openness to the room. An angel by Ben Ortega, a well-known folk carver from Tesuque, New Mexico, flies above a collection of antlers.

The sunset in the western sky pervades the dining room with the rose lights of evening. Each room in the home takes advantage of awesome views. At night the lights of Los Alamos can be seen twinkling in the Jemez Mountains.

A large semicircular porch acts as a platform for viewing the broad panorama beyond. A generous fireplace takes off the chill on summer evenings and turns the patio into an outdoor living space in use for many months of the year.

The living-room window frames a seemingly limitless vista. In contrast to the pale tones of the landscape is a striking Ganado-red rug made by Navajo Indians.

Talavera tiles, which derive their name from the pottery town of Talavera de la Reina in Spain, are made for the Southwest market in Puebla, Mexico, in a variety of colors and in lustrous glazes. Their elaborate interlocking Moorish designs enliven the bathrooms and kitchens of many Santa Fe homes. Here they frame a bathroom window.

AN INEVITABLE HOME

In 1930, Amelia Hollenbeck wrote to the young architect John Gaw Meem—who was later to become one of the leading figures in Santa Fe design—describing what she hoped to accomplish in the design of her home on Camino San Acacio on the outskirts of town: "You see, dignity and comfort permitting, I want something extremely informal that will let us amuse ourselves with old ways and old things, but may heaven preserve it from looking arty! I hope it will look merely natural and sort of inevitable." She outlined for Meem the important features of New Mexican architecture—doors, corbels, beams, and cupboards—and the architect incorporated elements from early New Mexican homes and churches, as well as from Indian pueblos, into the Hollenbeck house. The result is a veritable catalogue of original New Mexican architectural detail and design, a series of snug, secure small rooms that open onto monumental living rooms and long corridors.

Animals and the spirits they represent are important in the crafts of many Pueblo tribes. These owls and turkeys are by Acoma potters. The narrow long panes of the window behind the collection would originally have been filled with selenite, a translucent mineral that substituted for then-unavailable glass. The earliest recorded glass windows in New Mexico were placed in the Palace of the Governors on the Plaza.

One of the most curious aspects of the home is the mystery of Amelia Hollenbeck. Enigmatic and aloof, the young woman left her wealthy eastern family in the late 1800s and soon became an intermittent visitor in New Mexico. Eventually she made the decision to settle, but not long afterward she suddenly abandoned her home, leaving behind all of her possessions. The house remained empty of inhabitants but with every piece of furniture, every book, and every diary in place for over thirty years.

In the meantime, while the house lay vacant, Dr. Richard Cook and his wife, Mary Jean, had been looking for a special Santa Fe residence . When Amelia Hollenbeck died in 1969, Meem alerted the Cooks, and thereby set in motion an unusual relationship between the home and its new owners. Sifting through the untouched diaries, letters, and personal possessions of the young Hollenbeck, Mary Jean Cook realized the extraordinary nature of the woman whose house had become her own. Today she is biographer and editor of Amelia Hollenbeck's writings, as well as guardian of the legacy of her home.

The corner fireplace is often called a kiva fireplace because its round form mimics the shape of the kiva, the underground room used by Indians of the Southwest for ceremonies and meetings. A bean pot made of micaceous clay in the pueblo of Picuris is considered by many to be the best vessel for the slow cooking of pinto beans.

The painted door from the Peñasco area is one of the many antique architectural elements collected by Amelia Hollenbeck.

Above an *alacena*, a cupboard built into a hollow in the adobe wall, an old New Mexican shelf holds Hopi kachinas and Pueblo Indian pottery.

Spare and simply furnished, the main room of the early New Mexican home was often called the *sala*. In his design for the Hollenbeck home John Gaw Meem captured the spare formality of the early home, paying particular attention to the relationship between thick adobe walls and the weighty ceiling beams called *vigas*, supported by elegant corbels called *zapatas*. Amelia Hollenbeck collected many of the New Mexican furniture pieces in this room on her travels in the first decades of this century.

A front door in the shade known locally as "Taos blue" leads to an entryway of curving adobe walls, the hallmark of Santa Fe architecture.

The focal point of the kitchen, left almost as it was fifty years ago, is a magnificent old white enamel gas stove with a series of ovens. The stove boasts what must be the most valuable range hood in Santa Fe: the playful animals were painted by María Martínez, the most famous of the Pueblo potters. Like many New Mexican Indians, María Martínez considered Amelia Hollenbeck to be a close and valued friend, and she spent many hours in the Hollenbeck home—dancing, singing, and, on at least one occasion, painting.

The setting sun turns white walls to gold along a deep back *portal*, or porch. The *portal*'s beams and corbels were collected by Hollenbeck in the town of Bernalillo in the early twentieth century. Like the other ceilings and antique details of the home, they are among the most significant remnants of New Mexican architecture from the colonial period.

CORBELS

The facades and interiors of New Mexican buildings are often extremely simple, but ceilings—and their supporting elements, the corbels—consistently receive lavish attention to detail. Ceilings of *vigas* and *latillas* dominate the interiors, while on the exteriors, the most elaborate feature is frequently the corbel, found supporting the lintels of pueblo-style *portales*.

In early New Mexico, the corbel was one of the few decorated surfaces, wooden or otherwise. Sometimes carved in volute shapes, or embellished with chiseled or gouged notches, the corbels are also incised with delicate floral designs and then painted. Whether simple massive blocks of wood that emphasize the great weight of walls and ceiling, or intricately carved ornamental elements, the corbels are distinctive features of Santa Fe style.

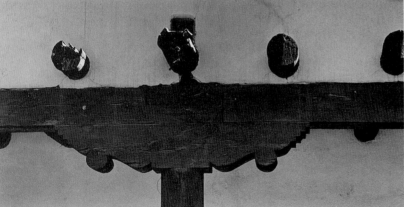

Right: A series of beams with fanciful corbels are used in this old garage. Long canales through the parapet carry water away from friable adobe walls.

A UNIQUE OPPORTUNITY

Ray and Judy Dewey, owners of a well-known gallery of Native American and Western art, spent many years seeking the proper setting for their outstanding collection of New Mexican artifacts. Impressed by the accomplishments of the Minges, whose Casa San Isidro is almost a museum of New Mexico's past, the Deweys began to accumulate doors, *trasteros*, *alacenas*, chests, and other Spanish colonial furniture and architectural details. The ultimate opportunity to complete this assemblage came in 1982, when the *vigas*, corbels, and bed molding from an eighteenth-century section of Santa Fe's Saint Francis Cathedral became available. The carved silver-gray pine sacristy ceiling—painted with natural pigments of soft reddish orange—would be the crowning feature of a large, dramatic room.

Finally, the Deweys found their setting—a nineteenth-century adobe home along the river on Upper Canyon Road.

The designer Jim Drum advised the Deweys that the living room of their new home was precisely the right proportions to accommodate their sacristy ceiling, and the Deweys began renovation. They are still at work on their home today, slowly adding to the authenticity and simple charm of their old adobe. "Sometimes when I come into my home," Judy Dewey said, "I still can't believe that it's ours."

An *alacena* holds the dining-room crockery; below, baskets are arranged on a rare example of painted New Mexican furniture.

At the front door, a combination of ancient timbers and contemporary reconstructions is a hint of the extraordinary woodwork found throughout the house.

Above: A big Santo Domingo dough bowl from the early years of the twentieth century rests on a shelf made from ancient carved timbers from the Acoma Pueblo. Below: San Isidro Labrador, a contemporary *santo* by the folk artist Frank Brito, on a sideboard in the dining room.

An early American hobbyhorse is an unusual example from the Dewey collection.

The ceiling of carved and painted corbels and *vigas* came from the sacristy of the parochial church of Saint Francis in Santa Fe, the present-day cathedral, and date from the mid-eighteenth century. The walls are painted with mineral pigments obtained from ancient quarries.

Punched tin in the country kitchen (above) allows air to circulate in cabinets but keeps out flying insects. Patterns are based upon early designs used in frames, sconces, and other tin household items made in the nineteenth century in Santa Fe. Below: The design surrounding the entry to the dining room, painted by María Romero Cash, a contemporary *santera*, painter of religious images, is based on early New Mexican *retablos*, religious folk paintings.

New Mexicans have a natural affinity for the colors and graphic design of the American flag. Stars, stripes, and tricolor combinations appear on every kind of furnishing, from Navajo rugs to Hispanic cupboards like the one shown here.

The Dewey home had belonged to Robert Woodman, a talented tinsmith whose work had been used to decorate many New Mexican businesses and homes in the 1930s and 1940s. Woodman had abruptly closed his shop in the late 1940s, and his workshop, still containing finished and unfinished examples of his tinwork, remained intact. Conveniently, the agent for the Woodman collection was Maurice Dixon, an artist who also works for the Deweys in their gallery. Dixon helped the Deweys select and install extraordinary examples of Woodman's craftsmanship.

In the kitchen, the corner fireplace with raised hearth is surrounded by reproductions of the type of colonial ironwork used by early New Mexican cooks.

Plains Indians beaded leggings accent an eighteenth-century Hispanic New Mexican pine chair.

Fires are built teepee-style in corner fireplaces and radiate a surprising amount of heat. The bedroom fireplace is in the territorial style. The *santos* on wall and windowsill are from New Mexico.

THE PUEBLO HOME

In 1926, Lois Field left Wyoming for Santa Fe to see what kind of trouble her parents had gotten themselves into. Her mother and father had set out for California and had discovered the bohemian charm of this small New Mexican town, rapidly becoming a colony of artists and writers. When Lois arrived she was appalled by the appearance of Santa Fe—"mud, mud, everwhere and everything is mud." She was equally startled by the inhabitants, who attended dinner parties in lumber jackets and opera dress, and she struggled with the pronunciation of Spanish street names. Gradually she not only recovered from the shock of entry into the new culture, she became entranced by its charm. By 1927 she had begun construction of her own adobe home. With an intuitive grasp of the unique features of Santa Fe life, Field based the plan of her house on the Indian pueblo. She had the adobes made on the site and enlisted the laborers to create special features.

Left: The multilevel facade of the house is reminiscent of Pueblo Indian communal dwellings. Right: The many outbuildings of the Field property provide ample opportunities for local crafts artists to display their talents.

SANTA FE STYLE EVOLVES

As director of the Museum of New Mexico's exhibition department, Jim Drum spent long hours designing and supervising installations of works of art. Still, he managed to find the time to renovate numerous homes for himself and his wife, and for selected clients, from historic adobe bungalows to framed stucco dwellings.

The Drum home on Artist Road presented a number of challenges. Strange claustrophobic passageways burrowed through the center of the house, which seemed to have been left untouched for decades. The Drums tore out interior walls, created new ceilings, installed copper tubing for radiant heating, and laid brick floors throughout. To highlight their

fine collection of folk art, they carved *nichos* into some walls and painted others to provide a dramatic backdrop for special pieces. Drum also used a series of *bancos* to line the walls, not only to provide comfortable seating, but also to break up the large interior spaces into smaller, functional areas.

The combination of *bancos*, the coved and fabric-covered ceilings, and the wall paintings gives to the Drum home a distinctive appearance that testifies to the special concerns of the people who created it.

Living areas in the open-plan home are defined by adobe *bancos* that link rooms as well as divide them. *Bancos*, which serve a practical function as benches, are often used to display Native American textiles.

Simple decorations, such as red chili *ristras*, emphasize the spare elegance of the home. In the living room, at the right, *bancos* and beams carve the large living space into smaller areas for different functions. *Nichos* house a collection of tribal, folk, and ethnic arts.

ADOBE ABODE

Katherine Otero built this adobe house in the pinyon-covered hills of Monte Sol overlooking the town of Santa Fe in the 1930s. Designed with a clear understanding and concern for the traditions of New Mexican building patterns, the Otero house features a long hallway that passes a series of bedrooms and is broken along the journey by steps and by *nichos*—small arched niches carved into the deep adobe walls.

Adobe walls lend themselves to built-in furnishings. Here deep-set windows act as a desk in one corner of a bedroom, and a *nicho* by the corner fireplace serves as a bookshelf.

Brick steps and a deep archway lead to a brilliant Ganado-red rug covered by a Plains Indians shield.

Among the arts of the Southwest Indians is the making of drums, used in ceremonial dances and admired by New Mexicans for their Old West appeal. This example is from Cochiti Pueblo. On the windowsill a figure of Juan Diego prays to the Virgin of Gualalupe. The rug is Navajo, in the popular pattern from Wide Ruins.

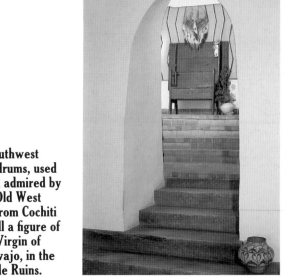

Unassuming pine beds follow traditional designs of New Mexican furniture. The bird pattern of the curtains was copied from the Navajo pictorial rug lying in front of the beds.

The present owner of the house has used these *nichos* to highlight a personal collection of kachinas from the Hopi and Zuñi, and figurative pottery, primarily from Cochiti Pueblo. The owner, formerly the manager of the trading post at Wide Ruins, Arizona, acquired her collection directly from the makers, some of the finest of Native American artists. She was also influential in the current revival of Navajo weaving, and the décor features many fine examples of Navajo rugs and blankets, with their broad geometric designs in vegetal colors.

Furniture is modest and secondary, and its simplicity gives prominence to the structure itself. The plain surfaces of the massive adobe walls are interrupted not only by the *nichos*, which emphasize the sculptural quality of the material, but also by a number of *alacenas*, wooden cupboards built into the earthen walls.

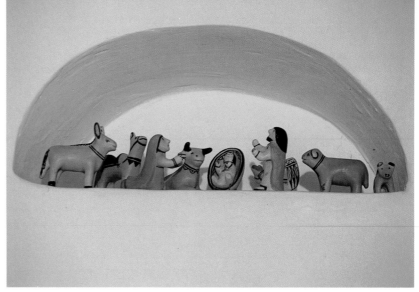

Functional little caves in the walls called *nichos*, often placed over doorways, highlight prized possessions—Hopi kachinas, Acoma Pueblo owls, and a ceramic Nativity scene from Cochiti Pueblo.

LIFE AS ART

Through his appreciation of New Mexican architecture, the painter Forrest Moses came to realize that his home was more than a place to live and work. Adobe walls, a chair, a flower, a sun-bleached ram's skull—these simple, beautiful objects not only created an aesthetically pleasing environment; they also became an artistic enterprise as crucial to Moses as placing pigment on canvas.

Over the years Moses transformed a rather insignificant little adobe into a rare work of art—a harmony of form, color, and space. He added a dramatic large studio that is a refreshing contrast to the small, comfortable rooms. Responding to the modest proportions of the living room, he selected simple classic furnishings, giving it an almost Shaker-like purity. Perhaps his greatest triumph is his creation of a garden from the dusty yard that surrounded the original home. In this tranquil setting are an effusion of blooms carefully chosen for color and proportion. The irises of a rare variety doubly grace Moses's home—as the flowers themselves and as the paintings they inspired.

Above: The adobe home on El Caminito, the Little Road, is reached by a cleverly stepped brick walk that echos the rectangular adobe wall around the front door. Below: Large double windows in the living room blend indoors with outdoors.

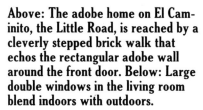

Light streaks through a carefully placed skylight, picking out the rough texture of the adobe wall and spotlighting a few carefully selected objects. Moses mixes found objects with handmade ones in changing exhibits.

Colonial Mexican doors open to the dining room. At the far end is a painting by Forrest Moses. The dining-room ceiling is pierced with skylights.

The small sitting room adjacent to the bedroom is simply furnished with Navajo rug, Mexican colonial bench, and the ever-present corner fireplace.

Precisely arranged Bosc pears in a lacquer dish testify to the aesthetic potential of the everyday.

The small proportions of the living room lend themselves to an intimate carefully arranged grouping of subdued furnishings, ideal for conversation.

A view through the bathroom, which transcends utility to become an important element in the visual landscape of the home.

A serene bathing area, with shower, hot tub, and small greenhouse.

Off the kitchen, a small study features the ubiquitous fireplace of adobe, here with particularly graceful curves.

91

ALONG THE SANTA FE TRAIL

The opening of the Santa Fe Trail in 1821 had far-reaching political significance for residents of New Mexico, and the influx of wagon trains brought changes in Santa Fe lifestyle, with a wealth of new building materials that transformed the primitive pueblo home into the modified style known as "territorial."

Left and above: Woodwork on doors and windows became more elaborate as American East met American West.

One of the most precious new materials, carried hundreds of miles over rough terrain from Missouri, was plate glass. The tiny windows of the pueblo home were soon replaced with attractive, double-hung paned windows. New Mexicans seem to have had an instant romance with Greek Revival and Queen Anne details, eagerly adapting these new elements to their adobe homes. With the introduction of tin sheeting in the late nineteenth century, the pitched roof—originally seen only in homes in the mountains, where snowfall is higher—became popular throughout the territory. Along with these new materials and styles came new house plans. Instead of tiny rooms around a central courtyard, the territorial home incorporated a central hallway and entry. The result of this seemingly incongruous

marriage of architectural styles is a remarkably pleasing and unique combination. The contrast of the thick, sensuous adobe walls with neat wooden trim, pediments, and shutters satisfies both the need for order and the love of the irregular and sculptural.

In the last five years, the territorial home, chiefly distinguished by its Greek Revival elements, has seen a resurgence of popularity. Modern proponents of the style admire its versatility. Older territorial-style homes are easier to acquire, since they far outnumber older pueblo homes, which were often adapted to the territorial style. In addition, the territorial style offers greater variety of interpretation: to the enduring simplicity of adobe, the territorial style adds sophistication and whimsy. Many homes feature flat roofs and plain Neoclassical designs around doors and windows, and atop *portal* posts. Others embrace the fancy gingerbread of carpenter Gothic, along with pitched tin roofs—an elaborate variation of territorial style that is sometimes called, partly in jest and partly with pride, Rio Grande Gothic. Among the most dramatic of recent innovations is the treatment of pitched roofs to leave beams exposed, creating a vaulted interior space. The adaptability of the territorial style, along with the its innate attractiveness, has been largely responsible for the evolution and preservation of Santa Fe's regional look.

A wagon wheel against a white territorial window frame—a reminder of pioneer days on the Santa Fe Trail.

NEOCLASSIC ADOBE

Territorial-style adobe homes offer their owners innumerable opportunities for interpretation—even some variations that seem at first to be alien to the Southwest. Don and Lila Madtson have found their home on Canyon Road to be the ideal setting for the display of their collection of American, English, and Spanish antiques. The Neoclassical features of the exterior of the house echo similar features of the furnishings. As with many territorial homes, the Madtson house seems to encourage eclecticism. The Georgian fire surround and eighteenth-century highboy, bought in the course of the Madtson's many trips to England, harmonize well with the ancient simplicity of the adobe. New Mexican Hispanic arts, as well as an impressive array of Pueblo pottery, have also found a place in the Madtson collection.

English, Spanish, and American antiques fill the living room. Visible through the doorway is a Connecticut fall-front maple and birch desk and a painting by the well-known New Mexican artist Fritz Scholder.

Above the door down a hallway hang nineteenth-century American rifles and hunting gear. The Spanish leather-covered chairs are draped with Navajo rugs. The pots on the table are from San Ildefonso and Santo Domingo Pueblos.

The plain Neoclassical facade is frequently finished with brick coping in territorial-style homes. The house faces the Santa Fe River, Santa Fe's main source of water for hundreds of years.

Like many Santa Fe homes, the Madtson adobe was in a semi-ruined state when they discovered it. The building had grown by stages over the centuries, and each new addition was an occasion to change the room level and vary the ceiling style. The Madtsons have gradually restored order to the house, preserving the central courtyard as a haven from the activities of Canyon Road.

During their years of renovation they discovered details about the house's history. A few of the older trees on the property indicate that it had its beginnings as a farm. The earliest known owners were José and Andrieta Martínez. Their daughter Miguelita lived in the house with her husband, Jesús González. When the Madtsons learned that the dining room of the house was called the Treaty Room, they imagined the signing of an historic document between Indians and colonists. They were surprised to learn that the treaty was the resolution of a feud between families, negotiated by Archbishop Lamy.

A small fireplace in the kitchen is called a Galisteo fireplace after the small community of Galisteo, where such fireplaces are common.

Santos, figures of saints, and carved crucifixes are examples of one of the earliest indigenous arts of New Mexico. Still carved by folk artists today, *santos* made in early Mexico and New Mexico are prized by collectors.

An outstanding collection of Pueblo pottery shows the virtuosity of the Pueblo painter. Eighteenth-century English and American furniture blends well with the Neoclassic adobe surroundings.

An early American high chest from New England serves well for the display of an impressive collection of American Indian baskets. Designs of baskets vary from tribe to tribe. Many Southwest Indians made baskets, from the Pueblos to the Apaches to the Pima, for use as bowls, trays, and jars. Today early Indian baskets are rare and used almost exclusively as display pieces, although contemporary baskets are found in kitchens and dining rooms of Santa Fe homes.

A SAWMILL TRANSFORMED

Before 1850, the New Mexican territory had no lumbermill and therefore no capability for mass-producing the wooden door and window frames that were essential to the developing taste for Greek Revival décor. The United States Army built the first sawmill in Santa Fe in that year, revolutionizing the plain facades of adobe houses with embellishments of milled lumber. Nearly seventy-five years later, that sawmill became the home of one of Santa Fe's most prominent artists, Randall Davey. When Davey arrived in Santa Fe with the painter John Sloan in 1919, he immediately decided to stay.

Davey found in his purchase the perfect opportunity to create his own style of living. The rambling outbuildings became a painting studio and stables for the horses he loved. The rushing waters of the river, which once turned the wheels of the mill, could be heard in the distance; the vast wilderness of the mountains beyond provided ample riding trails. Davey lived in his sawmill for forty years, producing portraits, nude studies, and racing pictures until his death in 1964.

Like many New Mexican artists, Davey scouted the region for New Mexican furniture, architectural details, and examples of indigenous art. Today the property is owned by the Audubon Society and remains as it was in Davey's lifetime.

The exterior of the Randall Davey home at the left shows the two-story facade with paintings by Davey flanking the front door. Downstairs, huge hand-adzed beams support the ceiling of the old mill. An old-fashioned saloon was created from the rocky cellar of the old mill. Doors from a cupboard inspired the design of the front of the bar and were incorporated into the back.

The drawing room on the second floor received many of Santa Fe's most prominent visitors.

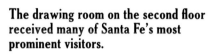

In Davey's studio in 1965 a painting of a racehorse—one of his favorite subjects—rests on the easel as it would have during the artist's lifetime.

VINTAGE STYLE, MODERN HOME

The inspiration for the classic territorial-style home of Patricia and Michael French came both from their growing appreciation of their adopted town, Santa Fe, and from a small old territorial home on their property. The little farmhouse behind the ancient pines was far too small to serve their active family, but the Frenches found so much to admire in it that they used its exterior appearance in the construction of their new home.

A long, deep *portal* extends across the facade of the three-year-old structure. Deeply recessed windows and territorial door and window frames recall the old adobes on which the house was modeled. The generous proportions of the rooms and hallways are modern, but the arched doorways and built-in cupboards are borrowed from traditional Santa Fe styles. Austere tiled floors and plain woodwork give the house a casual elegance, an excellent blend of the old and the new.

Entering through the graceful territorial-style front doors at the right, the visitor finds himself in a hallway that divides the functions of the house. Living areas and kitchen are to the right, and bedrooms are to the left. This arrangement of a broad central hallway giving onto a series of rooms was one of the innovations ushered in with the territorial period.

At the left built-in shelves in the Santa Fe style with bullet-carved moldings hold treasures from a collection of folk art. The ceramic vehicles are by Mexican folk artist Candelario Medrano. At the right double colonial Mexican doors at the end of the front entry hall can be closed for privacy. Skylights at the end of the ceiling of *vigas* and *latillas* bring natural light into the hall.

Double archways, decorated with Mexican tile, lead from the dining room to the kitchen. On one kitchen wall is a trio of *santos* painted by a contemporary folk artist. The curve of the doorways is reflected in the form of the raised-hearth fireplace. In the spirit of Santa Fe, the table is set with earthenware painted in country designs.

The archangel San Miguel tramps cheerfully upon the devil in a contemporary *santo* by the Santa Fean Anita Romero Jones. Behind the *santo* a small *nicho* carved from the adobe walls houses a group of old Mexican tiles of cherubim.

DOORS AND GATES

Regarded as necessary evils for keeping out cold and uninvited visitors, early doors were compact and heavy. Before the ready availability of iron and sawmill lumber in the mid-nineteenth century, the standard door was a hand-hewn panel of ponderosa pine hung by a simple wooden hinge called a pintle. These early doors are extremely rare, as are the later Rio Grande Gothic and folk territorial doors that are spirited interpretations of more staid Greek Revival and Queen Anne styles imported from the East. Local designs by New Mexicans working in mountain villages or small shops enlarge the repertoire with brightly painted folk doors further decorated with applied molding and openwork.

Along with these antique doors, which Santa Fe residents proudly display both inside and outside their homes, are the gates. The adobe walls that surround many homes now seem almost excuses to design a colorful gate. Whether delicate wrought iron, rough unfinished *latillas*, hand-adzed planks, or rows of spindles—Santa Fe has invented an infinite variety of gate forms.

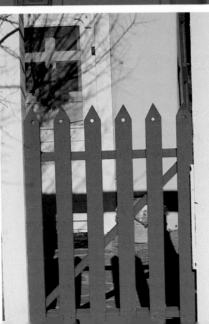

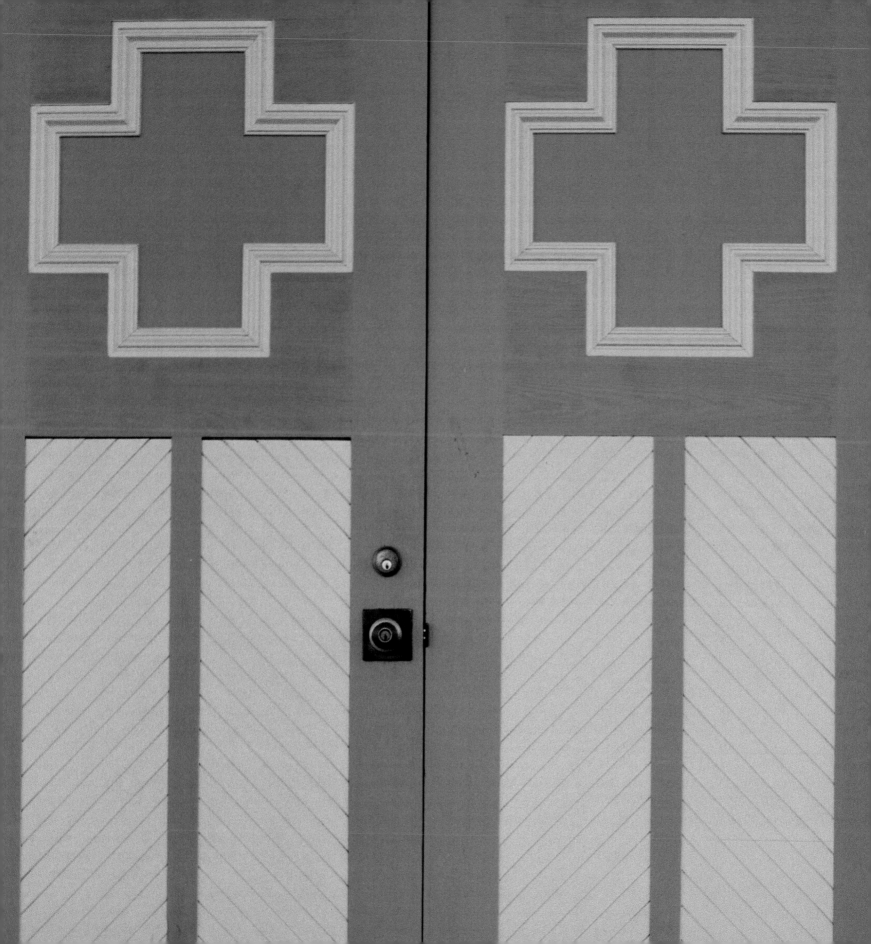

Historic photographs of doors and other architectural details serve as models for present-day woodworkers when the originals cannot be found. These fine examples of New Mexican doors were made of solid pine. At the left is a rare set of early double doors. Shown at the right top are a fine paneled door and a grilled door of turned spindles, probably made in the mid-eighteenth century. At the bottom are a nineteenth-century door in a diagonal pattern and a set of small paneled doors that may have served as the front of an *alacena*, a cupboard built into an adobe wall.

113

CARPENTER GOTHIC ADDITION

We had lived in our house for many years and were pleased with the privacy, the neighborhood, and the setting, but we were bored with the lack of style in the house itself. Our home was sound and uncluttered, but it had no distinctive features, and with a growing family, it was also too small. Moreover, we needed space not only for ourselves, but also for our collection of New Mexican and Mexican folk art. We had life-size sheep and bears to consider, ceramic prostitutes, and large Navajo rugs of scenes of the reservation. We also had a few prized pieces of New Mexican furniture of the territorial period that we needed room to display.

The solution was to opt for an addition that opened the room to the rafters in a large space that is both a living room and a gallery for our collection. The flat roof of the original house is set off by the pitched tin roof of the new addition, and the painted woodwork with the curves of carpenter Gothic—cutouts and finials—now enliven the once-bland exterior.

With our continuing interest in folk art, our collection seems to be constantly moving from my husband's, Davis Mather's, gallery to home and back again, as we find new favorites and introduce clients to old ones. Like many New Mexicans we frequently visit Old Mexico, where we collect, meet new artists, visit friends, and of course, eat. Our home reflects our continuing fascination with Mexico and our admiration for the vitality, color, and form of Mexican folk art.

Above: Whimsical folk art adds a humorous note to a formal dining room. The table is set with ceramic food by Josefina Aguilar of Oaxaca. Below: An open-ceiling living room, designed by Christine Mather and Sharon Woods, features a pine mantel in the territorial style.

An American flag rug by a Navajo weaver reflects a bold graphic style that typifies much of the art of the Southwest.

The corner cupboard in the dining room is painted green on the interior to contrast with the brightly colored woodcarvings from the Oaxaca province of Mexico. The mermaid duet is by Manuel Jimenez of Arrasola; a bandstand, cross, and Virgin were carved and painted by the Cruz family of San Felipe Tejalapa; and other animals are the work of Oaxacan artists.

115

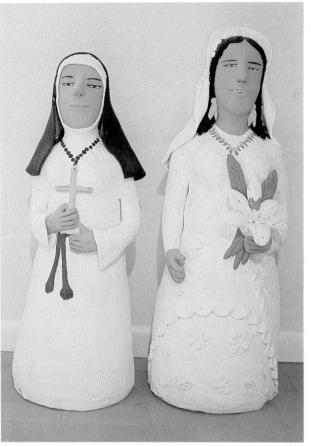

At the left a portrait of a cow above the mantel is a Navajo pictorial rug. The bulls are from villages around Oaxaca, Mexico. The zebra and wooden pig are by local folk artist David Alvarez. The two figures at the right are a bride and a nun by Josefina Aguilar of Ocotlán, Oaxaca. Made entirely of painted low-fired earthenware, these three-foot-high figures represent typical characters of Mexican villages.

Below: The Mexican water-jug rack of pine now holds a collection of woodcarvings by the well-known local folk artist Felipe Archuleta. The partially clad ceramic prostitutes, *nocturnas* as they are called in Spanish, are by Josefina Aguilar.

The two figures of Saint Anthony (San Antonio) are from Mesilla, New Mexico, and date to about 1840. A *retablo*, a wooden panel painted with a religious image for use in churches and village homes, was made in New Mexico about 1820 by the A. J. *santero*. The figure depicted is Saint Francis (San Francisco).

A more-than-life-size rabbit, carved and painted by Felipe Archuleta.

A small carved bird is typical of woodcarvings made by the Lopez family of Cordova, New Mexico.

A feline carving by Felipe Archuleta sports a Cheshire-cat smile.

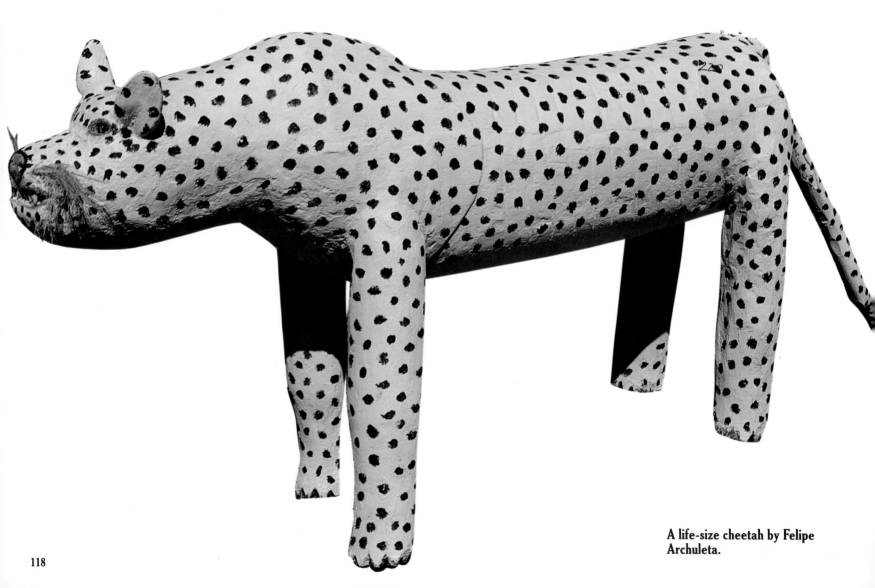

A life-size cheetah by Felipe Archuleta.

ANIMAL ARTS

What's the good of being famous if I don't be here much longer?" Felipe Archuleta, maker of life-size wooden animals, and irascible near-octagenarian, sums up the artist's dilemma. He also has a firm grasp of the nature of collectors and dealers: "Someday they'll go to my hole in the ground and say, 'where's my order?' " For all the fame and recognition he has received as the creator of folk art animals and as master for a group of followers, Archuleta stubbornly refuses to be bought out or in, to change his lifestyle, be gracious, or even friendly—or to compromise an art that seems to spring full-blown from a mysterious source in his psyche. A true original, he creates a wide variety of carved and painted wooden animals. In his younger days he tackled enormous projects, such as life-size giraffes and rhinoceroses. Current production is more modest in scale and less frequent. Followers Alonzo Jiménez, David Alvarez, and Felipe's son Leroy have developed personal styles using the same media, technique, and compositions originated by Felipe Archuleta.

A basket of carved and painted wooden melons by the folk artist Leroy Archuleta, son of Felipe Archuleta.

A skunk is one of the creatures in Felipe Archuleta's imaginative menagerie.

Above: Felipe Archuleta seated by one of his creations, a gorilla. Below: Leroy Archuleta with a hound he carved and painted in a style similar to his father's.

Carved and painted wooden snakes by Paul Lutonsky and coyotes howling at the moon by Alonzo Jiménez have captured the imaginations of Santa Fe residents and visitors. The snakes dangle over doors and windows, replace a framed picture over the living-room couch, and slither across *bancos*.

The old Hispanic home that Wells renovated had a deep *portal* and territorial features. By bricking the *portal* and patio, he created a grand outdoor living space.

The Hispanic weaving tradition is as old as the Spanish colonial occupation of New Mexico. Other kinds of needlework were also practiced in Santa Fe and neighboring settlements. The small New Mexican bed is covered with an embroidery by Policarpio Valencia, made in about 1910. Other *colchas*, embroidered textiles from New Mexico, can be seen on the floor and over the chair at the right. Religious imagery was particularly popular in Hispanic embroidery. The photograph was taken in 1937.

AN ARTIST'S RESTORATION

In 1935 the young artist Cady Wells bought a large Spanish adobe home in Jacona, New Mexico. With the help of architect John Gaw Meem, he restored the home to its original elegance. The interior he kept relatively simple, as a backdrop for his splendid collection of New Mexican Hispanic folk art and his landscape watercolors, which were bequeathed to the state of New Mexico after Wells's death in 1954.

Wells's intense interest in the rugged geometrical look of the New Mexican landscape and in texture and pattern are reflected in the juxtapositions of light and dark that distinguish the rooms of his home.

Wells was a warm and generous friend, and his home was the meeting place for Mabel Dodge Luhan, Georgia O'Keeffe, Raymond Jonson, and Martha Graham. During the 1950s photographers Ansel Adams, Laura Gilpin, Ernest Knee, and Tyler Dingee all recorded the unique charm of Wells's home.

A corner of the Wells home as it was in 1937, showing just a few examples of an important collection of New Mexican *santos* that he acquired. On the floor is a Rio Grande textile.

A deep *portal* with a brick floor set directly into the sandy soil. Artists like Cady Wells were influential in preserving and restoring Santa Fe.

CANYON ROAD ADOBE

The Spanish often granted land to early settlers and soldiers of the new colony. Colonel Vigil, who served with General Don Diego de Vargas, was the recipient of such a grant along the Santa Fe River in the 1690s. It served as the homestead for many generations of the Vigil family.

Today Peter and Francie Handler live in an adobe home that was once part of this Spanish Land Grant. The history of the house is typical of early Santa Fe: from a modest series of rooms, probably dating to the eighteenth century, the house expanded to include a number of rooms in the main house, along with outbuildings that the Vigils gradually sold as separate residences along Canyon Road. By the 1850s, the Vigils had yielded to the fashions of the territorial style, adding glazed windows, brick coping, and Greek Revival woodwork. The neighborhood around them also grew, so much so that it required its own local grocery store. The Vigils responded with Santa Fe's first drive-in store in the late nineteenth century, opening the double windows onto Canyon Road to sell dry goods and groceries to customers who pulled their buggies close to the house.

More household changes followed in the twentieth century. Perhaps the most satisfying of these involved incorporating an old goat shed into the living room, thereby bringing into the heart of the house the corbels and extraordinary long beam that had once framed a front *portal*. The *portal* was subsequently glazed, which increased the warmth and light in the house year round. High adobe walls bordering Canyon Road assured privacy.

Right: *Equipale* **leather-and-wood furniture of Mexico is found in many Santa Fe homes, both inside and out. Chilies, an essential ingredient of spicy New Mexican cooking, are left to dry from the beams of the small back** *portal.*

Above, left: Beams projecting beneath the territorial-style brick parapet are capped with a row of cow skulls.
Below, left: Wall painting is traditional among Spanish and Indian New Mexicans alike. The painting around the windows and the fireplace in the den are derived from patterns found on Pueblo Indian pottery.

To enhance their historic home, the Handlers have chosen furnishings and accessories with particular care. They have collected Indian pottery, Hispanic folk art, and Rio Grande textiles, as well as ceremonial artifacts from Zuni Pueblo. The fireplace combines a sitting area, a *banco*, with stepped-down shelves, which provide an excellent method of display for superb examples from their collection. The Handlers are especially concerned with rediscovering and preserving nineteenth-century wall paintings, originally a Spanish and Indian tradition. Around fireplaces and doorways, they have painted designs adapted from Pueblo pottery.

An ancient beam and corbel stretch across the front of the living room. Once part of the *portal*, the front wall has been glazed to take full advantage of the sun. The baked clay floor tiles, made in Saltillo, Mexico, in warm terra-cotta tones, are remarkably durable. Shelves on either side of the fireplace, stepped adobe projections, hold examples of Indian and Hispanic art.

126

SPANISH TEXTILES

Less well known than the Navajo weavings of the Southwest, but an equally important contribution to Santa Fe design, are the weavings of the Hispanic colonists of New Mexico. The Spanish introduced sheep to the Southwest, bringing with them not only the raw materials for the new art, but also a basic vocabulary of patterns that shaped Spanish and Indian textiles alike. The central diamond motif and jagged outlines, as well as simple stripes, lozenges, and leaves, all have their origins in the Iberian Peninsula or in Moorish designs.

Like the Indian textiles, the early Spanish cloth was produced for clothing and bedding, not for use on the floor. Only the long runners called *jergas* were meant to be walked on. Unlike the Indian textiles, which are made by women on upright looms, Spanish blankets were

This example of the weaving of Teresa Archuleta Segal hangs in her home in Española, New Mexico.

woven by men using the treadle loom, another Hispanic introduction into the New World. During the nineteenth century, these textiles were woven in volume and exported from New Mexico to Old Mexico and to California. Today called Rio Grande blankets, the Hispanic textiles of the eighteenth and nineteenth centuries are even less obtainable than their Indian counterparts, and are just as treasured. Contemporary weavers of Hispanic ancestry continue the tradition, weaving the old patterns in wool colored with natural dyes.

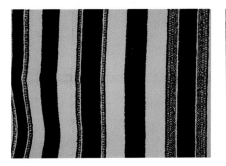 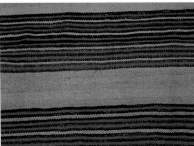 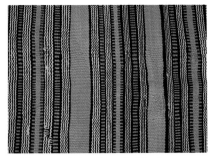

Bold, striped Rio Grande blankets are typical of the everyday textiles used in Spanish colonial homes in the nineteenth century.

On the loom a Rio Grande blanket by Teresa Archuleta Segal takes form. All of the wool is dyed by the artist, whose colors are the same natural dyes that were used by her ancestors.

On the back *portal* the bright white territorial-style trim of the windows contrasts with the straw-textured mud plaster of the walls. The antique cross is Mexican; the scaled-down cupboard is an old country piece.

A handblown glass cowboy hat rests on an adobe ledge. The Chambers home is plastered in true adobe (many homes today are built of more-economical adobe-colored cement), and gold tones of the straw used as a binding agent glint against the brown mud.

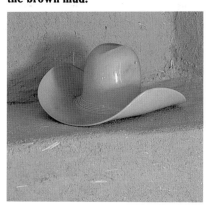

SANTA FE COUNTRY

An exciting aspect of Santa Fe style is that new homes are continually being designed to incorporate the traditions of Spanish, Indian, and territorial architecture, while exploring new ideas that are particularly well suited to a casual modern lifestyle. When Marion and Fred Chambers asked Victor Johnson to draw up plans for their new home in 1978, they wanted the best of Santa Fe design, but with enough room to accommodate visiting children and grandchildren.

The central organizing feature of the Chambers house is a *zaguan*, the central protected passageway that is the Spanish contribution to fortress architecture. The *zaguan* functions as both an indoor and an outdoor space, and also divides the Chambers house into public and private areas. The private side contains the master bedroom and bath and the kitchen, which serves as a separate living room. In addition to a large central table, the kitchen features a couch under a window that looks into the courtyard, and a corner fireplace. The public side of the house contains the living room and guest bedrooms. The *zaguan* not only separates the rooms according to function, but it also acts as a grand entryway and as a frame for one of the most spectacular views in Santa Fe. Beyond the *zaguan* is a *portal* that extends across the back of the house, from which the view can be enjoyed in summer.

The challenge for the modern Santa Fe architect is to preserve the thick walls of adobe that characterize the local style, while bringing light into interior spaces. In the hallway of the Chambers home that connects the guest bedrooms the designer added a skylight for illumination. Santa Fe-style *vigas* cross beneath the skylight, throwing a rhythmic pattern of shadows across the wall.

A big Taos sofa and a raised corner fireplace extend the use of the kitchen as a gathering place for the large Chambers clan. Large windows look onto the protected front courtyard.

Comfortable sofas upholstered in plain white fabric are a modern touch in an otherwise traditional adobe room. The striped textile on the far wall was woven by the Chambers's daughter.

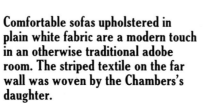

The Navajos learned to work silver from Mexican silversmiths in the second half of the nineteenth century. One of their best-known designs is the concho belt (after the Spanish *concha*, or shell), a series of silver disks connected with leather. Although not an Indian, Don Lucas (the Chambers's son-in-law) has made fine examples of this Indian-inspired design, which he displays in Santa Fe on Indian Market weekend.

Light from carefully placed skylights brightens a hallway that was constructed from lath, and doorways salvaged from a demolished room-and-board hotel of the nineteenth century.

Geraniums, though not indigenous to Santa Fe, thrive in its sunny, arid climate.

A dressing area off the master bedroom features a hatrack with a selection of headgear ready for summer outings.

In summer the back *portal*, which extends the entire length of the back of the house, becomes the main living area. A harvest table off the dining room accommodates the many family members who visit in summer months. In a house full of skylights, there is even one along the roof of this outdoor "room."

A stone pathway through the clover in the inner courtyard, the *placita*, leads to a door set in the wall.

Beyond the windows at the front of the house, a box of petunias. The front of the home is set into the hillside, and windows along that side are set at ground level, enhancing the sense of security provided by thick adobe walls.

A major feature of Santa Fe design is a contrast between the dramatic landscape and the intimacy and security of enclosed spaces. When the double doors of the Chambers' *zaguan* are flung open at either end, the house frames the vista beyond, seen here through the entry gate.

A Plains Indian beaded pouch from the Museum of New Mexico's extensive holdings of Native American art.

INDIAN ARTS

A series of spectacular concho belts from an important private collection hang from a New Mexican pine *trastero*.

Beaded pouches once contained their Indian owner's precious possessions. Now they are precious objects in themselves. The craftsmanship and design of these rare examples inspire contemporary Indian artists.

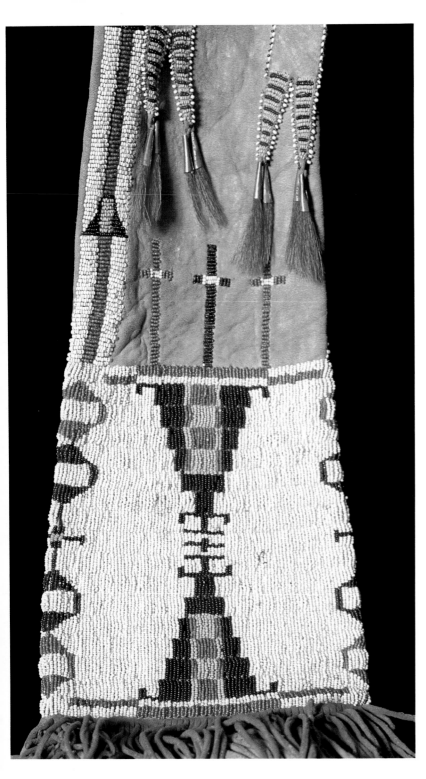

Simple beadwork pouches were once the common accouterments of Plains Indian men. Today they are rare artworks.

A casual collection of Indian jewelry hanging from a door provides instant adornment for their owner as well as a constant still life of Navajo jewelry.

A fine nugget of turquoise set in silver makes a dramatic ring. Distinctive New Mexican turquoise has been traded for many hundreds of years throughout the Southwest. Pre-Columbian sites in central Mexico have yielded objects made of turquoise mined in Cerrillos, New Mexico, just south of Santa Fe.

A series of contemporary concho belts by Don Lucas are in designs based upon Navajo jewelry.

PORTALES

The *portal*, or porch, of a Santa Fe home is often the most important clue to the character of the home and its owners. Deep and generous, both defending and welcoming, the *portal* is the Southwest's most profound contribution to architecture. Stretching across both the back and the front of many homes, *portales* have architectural details that are in keeping with the overall style of the home. For example, *portales* of pueblo-style homes are supported by carved corbels and beams of early New Mexican buildings, while those of the territorial home have beams and posts as their supports. Lining the *portal* are daybeds, wicker furniture, old benches, wrought-iron furniture, old New Mexican chests and *trasteros*—a variety of comfortable and practical furniture for outdoor living. The back walls of the *portal* are frequently painted white in order to reflect light into the deep space. It is here also that stenciled and painted designs and decorative tile can often be found.

Left, top row: Dorothy McKibben home and wall paintings on *portal* of the Mabel Dodge Luhan home, Taos, New Mexico. Middle row: New Mexico street scene, about 1930, and *portal* on Canyon Road. Bottom row: *Placita*, Santa Fe, early twentieth century, and *portal*, Las Vegas, New Mexico, about 1930. Right: back *portal* on an old Santa Fe home.

SUNLIGHT ALONG THE CAMINO

The architect John McHugh designed and built his two-story adobe in the early 1940s, long before passive-solar heating had become an essential feature of homes in the Southwest. Using enormous old windows from an 1840s Santa Fe boardinghouse, he designed an overscaled living room that is always filled with light.

The present owners were attracted to the home because of its generous proportions and quality of light: sunlight not only brightens the rooms; it also heats the brick and adobe of floor and walls. The second floor, reached only by an exterior stairway, is the children's domain. An ample country kitchen added by the owners meets all the requirements of the serious cook and adds a touch of Santa Fe. The cabinets mix elements borrowed from New Mexican furniture and from Mexican and American country cupboards.

Above: A wide-open country kitchen with broad plank pine floors and warm pine cupboards. Below: Fireplaces appear in almost every room. The mantle of the main fireplace in the living room is of pine, seen in many Santa Fe territorial-style homes. The ceramic candleholders are very early rare examples from Metepec, Mexico.

Doors and transom were salvaged from a Santa Fe boardinghouse. Cupboards are one of the favorite pieces of furniture in Santa Fe and can be used for a variety of purposes, replacing closets and here storing linens.

In the master bedroom, above the fireplace (which conveniently faces the bed), is a painting by the late Native American artist T. C. Cannon.

The brick floors of the entry hall are covered with Navajo rugs. The corner fireplace has an asymmetrical opening, indicating a renovation or improvement of the past.

147

CUPBOARDS

Santa Feans love their cupboards, perhaps because an adobe home never has sufficient closet space or shelving. In Spanish colonial times cupboards, called *trasteros*, along with other furniture, were imported into New Mexico along the Camino Real.

The pie safe was made in the late nineteenth century in Galisteo, New Mexico. A collection of ceramic, tin, and wood vehicles brought from Mexico are on top.

A whimsical Mexican cupboard in the kitchen holds a colorful collection of American majolica pottery from the nineteenth century.

A Mexican cupboard filled with Mexican earthenware and handblown glasses.

An early American country cupboard with its original blue paint holds American majolica.

149

CEILINGS

Ceilings have always been important decorative as well as structural elements in Santa Fe architecture, providing a textural contrast to the smooth adobe. *Vigas* are the first part of the ceiling to be installed: these are the massive timbers that span the width of the room. Over these are laid the *latillas*, stripped saplings arranged either in straight rows or in a herringbone pattern.

In Santa Fe homes today these basic building blocks have been reinterpreted in seemingly endless variations. In territorial-style ceilings, the *vigas* are often squared off and finished with a chaste edging or channel. Coved ceilings are created by plastering between the *vigas*, and contemporary ceilings incorporate skylights. Sometimes a heavy ceiling may require the use of corbels, sometimes called *zapatas*, to distribute the weight more evenly; a bed molding placed high on the wall sometimes supports the ceiling as well.

Left: *Vigas* and *latillas* in a dramatic ceiling from the monastery near Abiquiu, New Mexico.
Right, above: Square *vigas* and a split-cedar ceiling in Santa Fe. Below: Folk paintings on the ceiling at San José de Gracia Church in Trampas, New Mexico, and a ceiling of *tablas* made of split cedar. Far right: Railings, posts, corbels, and beams from a *portal* at the De la Peña House in Santa Fe.

HACIENDA AND RANCH

When settlers from the eastern United States began arriving in New Mexico in the mid-nineteenth century, they encountered a new idea in cattle raising, running cattle on the open range. Many details of ranch life were derived from the traditions of the Mexican cowboy—the vaquero—and first appeared north of the Rio Grande in New Mexico.

Left: A collection of tools against a *portal* wall. Above: A pitched tin roof and plain white posts dress up the ranch facade.

The first New Mexican ranchers had to endure a number of hardships. Indian raids—from the Apache, Comanche, and Navajos—continued well into the nineteenth century. The basic design of the *hacienda*-style ranch reflected the pressing need for protection from these attacks. Domestic tasks could be performed safely in inner courtyards with high adobe walls, which also guarded animals at night. As country life became less dangerous in the late nineteenth century, the ranch house opened out, spreading laterally to admit light into every room. The increased availability of lumber as a building material inspired a new rustic home that was more like the wooden homes of the East than the haciendas of Mexico. Broad, deep porches—*portales* in Spanish—provided a comfortable resting spot at the end of a hard day's labor.

Peaceable interaction with Indians through commerce was also a feature of rural New Mexican life, and the reservation trading post became an important means of transmitting goods along with the cultural ideas behind them. The New Mexican settlers soon came to appreciate the beauty and functionality of Indian rugs and pottery, and these became an important feature of their homes.

Weathered wood of an old shed provides background to an equally weathered assortment of tools collected around the ranch house, where every useful object, no matter how old, might one day be needed.

Lintels, corbels, and beams of cotton-wood form the *portal* of the inner courtyard, which encloses a garden of native flowers.

A LIFETIME DEVOTION

Although New Mexico can claim some of the earliest settlements in the United States, few examples of individual structures remain because of the friable nature of adobe. The sun-dried bricks are easily destroyed if exposed to moisture, and a house so damaged was often abandoned rather than repaired. This was apparently the case with the large hacienda and group of outbuildings in the small rural town of Corrales that Dr. Ward Minge and Shirley Minge purchased in the 1950s. Casa San Isidro, the name they gave to the home they constructed on the foundations of a former grand hacienda (named after the patron of a small church that stood a few yards from their front gate), is one of the finest examples of the early Hispanic house style.

The Minges devoted themselves to the scholarly study of domestic architecture and daily living in eighteenth- and nineteenth-century New Mexico. They attempted to restore the original functions to the main rooms around the courtyard—the *sala*—that was used as the ceremonial meeting place or great hall, the small formal parlor that was added in the nineteenth century, a room for weaving, and even a small chapel, or *oratorio*. The Minges strove for accuracy in every detail: they acquired ceilings, windows, beams, doors, and even the tools used to fashion these architectural elements. They also accumulated one of the finest collections of Hispanic folk art and crafts, including carvings and textiles that are rare simply because of their ordinariness.

Left: A territorial-style window is one of the many architectural features salvaged from an old building and brought to Casa San Isidro. Right: A *portal* from the mid-nineteenth century extends down one side of the courtyard to the double door entryway of the *sala*, the main living room.

The *sala* of the hacienda was the meeting and entertaining room. It could accommodate numerous guests and was often the site for the household fiesta. The sparse but large-scale furnishings of this room are true to the type of furniture that would have been found in grand eighteenth-century *sala*.

With the rising fortunes of Hispanic families in the nineteenth century and the newly opened avenues for trade, families began to acquire such luxuries as grand pianos and golden harps.

A handsome New Mexican *trastero* of the nineteenth century in the *sala*. Large windows look to the central courtyard, or *placita*, beyond.

The walls of the dining room were tinted pink with pigments found in local soils. On the floor is a *jerga*, the common floor covering of the Hispanic hacienda. All of the furniture found in these rooms was made in New Mexico during the eighteenth and nineteenth centuries.

The kitchen of Casa San Isidro is dominated by a handsome blue stove acquired from the mountain village of Chimayo. The "muddler," jug, cup, and bowl on the table are used in the preparation of Mexican-style hot chocolate. In the Spanish colonial world, chocolate was highly prized. Often kept under lock and key, it could be offered instead of cash in commercial transactions, and it is not uncommon to find it listed among other valuables in wills of the colonial period.

Around a large grain chest are sifters and *metate y mano* used in the preparation of grains. The simple window made entirely of wood without metal hinges is called a *zambullo*.

RANCH LIFE PRESERVED

Located in the wetlands of La Cienaga, just south of Santa Fe, the Rancho de las Golindrinas (The Swallows Ranch) was a working ranch that served as a stage stop between Albuquerque and Santa Fe in the nineteenth century. Today it has been transformed into a living museum of Hispanic village life. A variety of adobe and log buildings illustrates the humble architecture of rural New Mexico. They are used by artisans who exhibit the early crafts of weaving, black-smithing, rope making, and baking in the outdoor beehive ovens called *hornos*.

Within these buildings, the furnishings are much as they were in early New Mexican homes. Shepherd's fireplaces for heating and cooking, packed earthen floors, simple wooden bedsteads and mats for sleeping offer the bare minimum of functional requirements.

Each of the buildings was brought to the ranch or built on the site to illustrate the various vernacular architectural styles found in New Mexican villages. In addition, they are home and workplace for the industries and crafts of early New Mexican frontier life.

Even in towns, bedrooms were almost an unknown luxury until the nineteenth century. Before that time, sleeping mats made of handspun cloth stuffed with wool or straw and animal furs were used as bedding at night and were rolled up and placed along the walls for seating during the day. With the opening of the Santa Fe Trail, new styles in furniture arrived, and local craftsmen began to fashion little spindle beds and daybeds for their clients.

The kitchen, with its large open fireplace for cooking, was a welcome and friendly room that dominated the New Mexican *ranchero*. Drying herbs and boiling beans filled the air and a pinyon-wood fire warmed the adobe walls.

Frontier life by necessity created a great self-reliance and a harmony with the environment that is reflected in the interiors of early homes. Every object at Las Golondrinas is hand-made, functional, simple, and in tune with the setting. The pine furniture follows centuries-old traditions of Hispanic woodworking and is so conservative in style that it has often been compared to medieval European furniture.

A big *trastero* (cupboard) and a few chairs may have been the finest possessions of the country home. Stenciled or painted walls and other decorations brought rustic elegance to the "formal" rooms.

An old *santo* in a *nicho* set into an adobe wall.

CHAPELS

Within Hispanic households it has long been the practice to reserve a special area of the home or a separate room or building for the celebration of religious activities. Home altars or private chapels, *oratorios*, were once found in every home or village. These personal shrines contained representations of popular saints, *santos*, made by local artisans.

Oratorio of Eulogio and Zoraida Ortega, Velarde, New Mexico.

Our Lady of Guadalupe, a carved and painted *santo*, was made by José Rafael Aragón, a folk artist working in the mountain villages north of Santa Fe during the nineteenth century.

Many deserted churches dot the New Mexico landscape. One *oratorio* in ruins on a Santa Fe hillside is brought back to life with neon outlines around doors and windows. The interior of another abandoned church is at the right.

George Lopez of Cordova, New Mexico, holds a *santo* of his making, about 1935.

Below: Taos Pueblo, one of the best-known pueblo communities, is a multilevel composite of communal houses on the edges of the town of Taos. San Geronimo Church dominates one side of the pueblo's plaza.

Left: New Mexico's most-visited shrine, the Santuario in Chimayo, was built in the early 1800s by the Abeyta family. Thousands of pilgrims travel to Chimayo during Holy Week before Easter.

169

HOME ON THE RANGE

The sheep farmers came first, followed by cattlemen. Finally, after the opening of the railroad in 1879, Anglo farmers immigrated to New Mexico to work the land, sometimes suffering great difficulties as drought ruined the crops they had grown successfully in the more temperate climate back east. Some adapted their methods to dry-farming crops that could survive harsh growing conditions, but today most farmers in New Mexico employ irrigation.

New Mexico became a state in 1912 and shortly thereafter began to attract visitors who had more interest in traveling than in settling in the region. By the 1920s and 1930s Santa Fe's unique combination of climate and culture had made it an attraction for the hardier tourist, and residents soon developed means of housing and entertaining these new guests.

Dude ranches followed close on the heels of the real thing in New Mexico. At Tent Rock Ranch in the 1930s, dudes gathered for a ride through the tall ponderosa pines in the mountains. Logs were the primary building element inside and outside the mountain ranch. Guests bunked in narrow beds made of stripped branches, read by the light of a jug lamp, and soothed their eyes on Western scenes hung on log walls. The real clues to the rustic life are the flashlight and slippers on the nightstand, ready for any necessary trips into the night.

The dining hall at Pop Shaffer's Hotel in Mountainair, New Mexico, is a clutter of Pueblo-Deco Indian motifs, Navajo rugs and doilies on stick furniture, and bizarre root animals made by Pop. Carved at his ranch, Rancho Bonito, at the edge of town, the animals and decorations entertained guests who traveled to the remote town along the early highways that crossed the country. From Mountainair they could visit the earliest missions in America at Quarai, Abo, and Gran Quivera—sixteenth-century outposts of the Spanish empire.

A homesteader's cabin from around 1915 is a stark contrast to the dude ranch and travelers' Western rest stop of twenty years later. Poor farmers claimed the West at the expense of their toil upon the land. Just a few decades separate the hard reality of Western life from the romantic vision that it was to become.

Pat Garrett, Sheriff William Brady, Governor Lew Wallace, and the most famous outlaw of all—Billy the Kid—gave the West its reputation for colorful characters and adventure. Growing up in the rough mining town of Silver City, New Mexico, in the 1870s, Billy the Kid was caught up in the range wars that raged across Lincoln County south of Santa Fe. He and his gang rustled cattle, killed a sheriff, and terrorized ranchers. John S. Chisum ultimately organized his fellow cattlemen and hired a new sheriff in 1880, and the outlaw, whose real name was William H. Bonney, was gunned down by Pat Garrett at Fort Sumner, New Mexico, in 1881. Today the territory that Billy the Kid made legend retains much of its turn-of-the-century character. The adobe and wood houses and town facades of the Wild West are preserved at Mesilla and Lincoln, mementos of a tumultuous past.

Ranch buildings and corrals were constructed of the same adobe, timber, and plaster as buildings in town, but often with the addition of logs for walls and heavy gates, and stone for foundations and fireplaces.

Log cabins are seen more frequently in New Mexico in the mountains, where evergreen forests make lumber the most readily available building material. Inside the Jesus Baca Ranch on Cow Creek in the Pecos Wilderness, the walls are of cedar. With its Navajo and Hispanic textiles and comfortable furnishings the Baca Ranch was—and is today— a welcome resting place for world-weary urban dwellers.

175

A WRITER'S PARADISE

I wish I was in Santa Fe at this moment," wrote D. H. Lawrence in 1923, affirming a love affair with New Mexico that had begun two years earlier, when he accepted the invitation of the patron of the arts Mabel Dodge Luhan to visit her in Taos. Lawrence and

After his death in 1930 in Venice, Lawrence's wife, Frieda, had a chapel built on the New Mexico property to pay homage to Lawrence. His remains are buried in this memorial.

Responding immediately to the spirit and culture of New Mexico, Lawrence painted the bison and other animals that appear on the adobe walls and built some of the furniture in the rustic New Mexican style. Although his novels, such as *Women in Love* and *Lady Chatterley's Lover*, have long been acknowledged as major literary works of the twentieth century, Lawrence's paintings have only recently attracted critical attention.

his wife, Frieda, spent nearly three years, off and on in the 1920s, in New Mexico, and his memories of the peaceful life, along with the rituals and dances of the Indians, profoundly influenced his writing for the rest of his life.

In exchange for the manuscript of *Sons and Lovers*, Luhan gave Lawrence an old homesteader's ranch outside of Taos. There he and Frieda enjoyed some respite from their stormy life together, in a log and adobe cabin.

"For greatness of beauty I have never experienced anything like New Mexico," D. H. Lawrence wrote. The chair was made and painted by Lawrence.

RAISE HIGH THE ROOF BEAMS

An important Santa Fe builder, Betty Stewart has constructed a number of handsome houses characterized by excellent views, grand scale, and an overall spirit of generosity and comfort. Her trademark—the revival of the pitched tin roof with an innovation of exposed beams in the ceiling—has created controversy in a town that has codified pueblo and territorial architecture into law, but the large open spaces of her rooms have inaugurated a new era in the revitalization of Santa Fe style.

In her own home, thick walls of double adobe built with five inches of air space between each course muffle noise and help to insulate from heat and cold. The high ceilings, ancient beams, deep reveals around handsome windows, and broad *portales* suggest a freedom especially suitable for country living.

Betty Stewart comes from an old New Mexico ranching family, and she keeps many reminders of ranch life in her new home. A large Navajo rug draped on a bench in the hallway off the living room was once part of her grandfather's bedroll. Horse gear and rifles hang on and over the pine bench. In every room, Stewart has kept the thick adobe walls, pierced by arches and windows, along with fireplaces and handmade furniture in the Santa Fe tradition.

Exposed beams in the living room and kitchen, crucial to the open-plan design, are salvaged elements from old buildings.

From the living room toward ancient double doors to the kitchen is the skylit atrium entrance hall, decorated with racks of antlers, a fountain, and potted trees.

A rare New Mexican *santo* of the Virgin, made in the Cordova area about 1840, found objects, and Indian artifacts.

Left: The thickness of the adobe walls can be seen in this view through a door into a small hall. Few contemporary homes have walls as deep as these. Above: A folk painting.

Lorenzo Hubbell changed the direction of Navajo weaving by encouraging women to make enormous rugs—such as the one he holds in this 1890 photograph—instead of the wearing blankets they wove for their own use.

The interior of Hubbell's home in Ganado, Arizona, taken in 1890, shows his enormous collection of Indian baskets, which he displayed by nailing them to walls and ceilings.

Wool and weaving introduced a cash economy to the Navajo reservation, creating a market for the mass-produced goods that could be purchased in the trading posts. The photograph was taken in 1949.

Part of the old Hubbell residence had a sod roof.

TRADING POST AT GANADO

Situated just across the New Mexican border in Arizona is the trading post built and operated by Lorenzo Hubbell on the Navajo reservation in the late nineteenth century. Until fairly recently many of the roads on the vast Navajo nation were almost impassable for much of the year because of rain and snow, and the Navajos had to depend on the trading-post system for their manufactured and canned goods. In exchange, they offered examples of their native crafts— silver jewelry and woven blankets—which were in turn sold to tourists or shipped back east by the traders.

Hubbell particularly encouraged the women weavers to refine their art, both in technical skill and in design. The walls of his trading post, which is now a National Historic Site, are lined with painted sketches of chiefs' blankets and other traditional patterns. Piles of rugs, made by contemporary Navajo weavers, are offered for sale as they were in Hubbell's day.

Outside the Tze-He-Lih trading post, cowboys and Indians pose before a group of outstanding Navajo rugs in 1890. Collectors today would welcome the opportunity to own one of these handsome examples, now rare and exceedingly expensive. Once traded as tourist goods, Navajo rugs are now part of many museum collections.

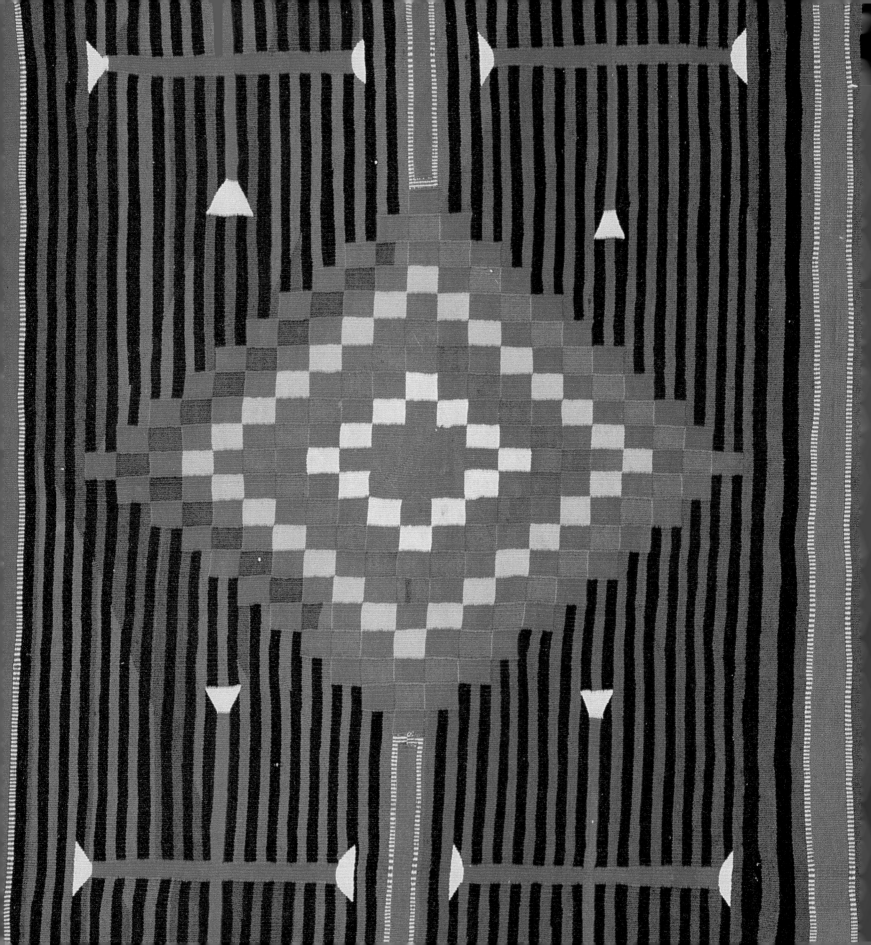

FINISHED IN BEAUTY: NAVAJO WEAVING

The Navajo rug, with its bold colors and graphic designs, has become a symbol of the American West. It originated in the early years of the eighteenth century as a blanket worn by both men and women. Most scholars believe that the Navajo were taught weaving by the Pueblo Indians, who used a native cotton, but the Navajo soon surpassed their teachers, especially after the Spanish brought sheep—and thus wool—to the region.

Left: A fine example of a chief's blanket. Right: Variety of pattern and color in Navajo weaving.

FIREPLACES

No Santa Fe room looks complete without a fireplace. On winter nights the brisk Santa Fe air fills with the fragrant, distinctive aroma of burning pinyon wood, which is stacked vertically in the adobe fireplace. The sturdy, efficient corner fireplace is the most common design—one rarely seen in other parts of the country. It sometimes has a raised hearth in order to project more heat into the room and to warm those seated at adjacent *bancos*. A more elaborate type of fireplace, called the shepherd's fireplace, has a broad, deep shelf above an open hearth.

Plastering both inside and out was done entirely by women. This Spanish woman is creating a corner fireplace.

A turn-of-the-century Santa Fe resident enjoys the solitude and intimacy of her fireplace.

Once a warm sleeping platform for the shepherd, the shelf is often used today for the display of prized Indian ceramics. The *paredcito* is a corner fireplace with a small, low wall that acts as a room divider. Outdoor fireplaces, and the common baking fireplace, the *horno*, are also seen frequently in a community that spends much of its time in the open air.

An elegant fireplace created by early Santa Fe artist Carlos Vierra, in about 1918. Vierra used bent cedar branches that were then plastered over to reveal just a part of the wood in creating this hood for a corner fireplace.

A VIEW TO THE FUTURE

Santa Fe's architectural style has been developing for over four centuries. Despite efforts to codify certain aspects of Santa Fe style through zoning laws and community pressure, design has continued to grow and change, reflecting the fundamental adaptability of this vernacular form of building and its suitability to the American Southwest.

Above: A rock protrudes into the living room of the Boulder House. Right: The modern version of the adobe home.

Native American builders gave to the Southwest an unusually rich vocabulary of house forms that accommodated large groups in a communal lifestyle. Condominiums, which have sprung up in every American community like the ticky-tacky boxes of the famous folk song, are found in Santa Fe too, but here their continuous plan mimics the compact, joined housing of Spanish and Native American tradition.

Most housing in Santa Fe, including condominiums, pays more than symbolic homage to the sun. Solar construction dominates contemporary building, and many older structures have been updated with the introduction of solar technology. Many of the earliest passive-solar homes built in the United States are in the Santa Fe area, as are the leading proponents of this clean, economical system for heating and lighting. Until very recently, scientists and the construction industry alike doubted the efficacy of solar heating. Now other areas of the United States are trying to catch up with experiments performed in the Southwest.

The legacy of native building materials fostered the trend toward energy-efficient housing. Adobe, the primary building block of the

past, is often chosen for contemporary homes as well. Although its initial installation is costly, the expense is justified over time, not only because of the undeniable attractiveness of the natural material, but also because of adobe's insulating property, which not only makes the home warmer in winter and cooler in summer, but makes it quieter year round.

Progressive architecture, by opening homes to the light, has also opened them to the natural beauty of the Southwestern landscape. Once considered hostile and barren, unprotected from the elements and attacks by animals and unfriendly neighbors, the land of New Mexico is now regarded as a great resource—by those who live here and by those who sample its treasures only briefly.

The Santa Fe sun filters through an ingenious awning of a contemporary home.

THE LEGACY OF PUEBLO BONITO

Named the Desert Flower by its designer and builder, this one-year-old home is the result of a deep impression made on an eleven-year-old boy by the ancient Anasazi ruins of Pueblo Bonito in New Mexico's Chaco Canyon. When he first visited the site forty years ago, he was fascinated by the interrelationship of the many small rooms that made up the Indians' living quarters and their religious rooms, called kivas: "I made my first adobe model that very evening."

Pueblo Bonito, thought to date to as early as 950 A.D., is laid out in a semicircle, which became the basic plan for the Desert Flower, located in the Tierra Mesa section west of town. The round wall projects into the hillside behind the house; the flat side, with its solar greenhouse, faces south. The influence of the Anasazis is seen not only in the materials used and in the overall plan, but also in the way that the contours of the house echo the natural shape of the hillside and the curve of weathered wood used in lintels and beams. Windows and doors are cut to follow the curves of the walls. These organic lines soften the severity that distinguishes much of modern architecture.

Few houses maximize the fluid properties of adobe as well as Desert Flower. From the greenhouse with its custom-fitted glass panels to the walkway that follows the sinuous contour of the hillside, the house seems to expand and contract organically to match the environment. The Desert Flower is a manmade cave— one of the most unusual structures in Santa Fe.

Few architects in the West remain unaffected by the practicality and functional beauty of the Anasazi construction methods, and elements of their dwellings are found in almost every Santa Fe home—even if it is only a ladder on a garden wall, once an essential feature of the vertical early pueblo village and still found in pueblos today. The Desert Flower preserves the sense of ceremony and mystery of these early dwellings.

Left: Deep adobe *bancos* are the only furniture in the living room.
Right: The bedroom entry is framed by natural timbers gathered nearby.

A MODERN GENIUS INTERPRETS ADOBE

The great twentieth-century architect Frank Lloyd Wright designed one adobe house, which he called the Pottery House both because of the materials to be used in its construction and because of its unique bowl shape. Wright began the commission in 1941 for an El Paso couple, but the home was built only after plans were purchased from the Frank Lloyd Wright Foundation for construction in Santa Fe that began in 1984. Although more than forty years have elapsed since the house was designed, the Pottery House is a remarkable contemporary structure on the Santa Fe landscape.

Wright liked to incorporate into his houses the soothing sight and sound of water; the Pottery House features deeply recessed showers, waterways, and a curved pond in an ovoid central courtyard, which mimics the lines of the house.

Many interior features follow this ovoid as well: unusual windows in several of the rooms not only follow the exterior contours; they also appear to be eyes from which to view the landscape beyond. The round main fireplace, which fills one side of the curved living room, resembles an Indian pot.

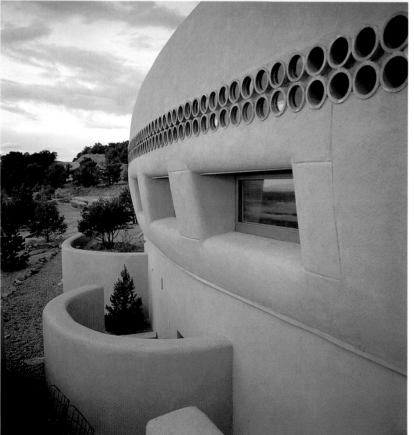

The flowing outlines of the Pottery House are repeated in walls, pools, and doorways. Set high in the Santa Fe foothills, it commands an extraordinary view of mountains and city.

Wright designed furniture for many of his homes, but Pottery House plans did not include such details. The couple who lives in the recently built home has brought with them Mexican colonial furniture, which blends and contrasts with the modern setting.

Spaces carved into the thick adobe walls provide not only display areas for special objects such as this green glazed Spanish olive jar of the colonial era, but also a visual link between rooms. This perforation in the adobe wall passes from a seating area to the living room.

Extraordinary fit and finish characterize the Wright approach to design. The series of windows in this den uses specially cut glass. Low horizontal windows below give onto the broad panorama that lies just outside the windows.

A curved connecting hallway faces toward patio, pool, and a view of mountains and sky. Many Santa Fe residents are attracted to the geometric designs of oriental carpets, which resemble Native American weavings in their bold abstractions and bright colors.

PUEBLO INDIAN POTTERY

Pottery was an important part of Southwest culture in pre-Columbian times and was produced in great quantity in the pueblos. Introduced before 500 A.D. along with the distinctive architectural forms of the Pueblo Indians, pottery making is one of the oldest continuing arts of the Americas. Most of the highly valued early pottery was made for specific utilitarian purposes, but the forms and decorations go far beyond the merely functional. The carefully controlled painted designs of geometric and animal patterns have continued to enrich the vocabulary of the contemporary potter. Today collectors may plan their homes specifically to show off their Indian ceramics.

Each pueblo village has its own distinct pottery forms. The ancient firing method, handed down from mother to daughter (and now often from mother to son), is a delicate one, and many fine pots can be lost during the process. Many designs and methods of manufacture are hundreds of years old. The traditional designs reflect the complex cosmology of the Pueblo religion as well as a kinship with the forces of nature. Contemporary potters use time-honored designs as a starting point for new interpretations.

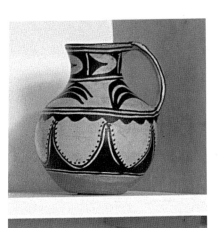

The storyteller is by Cochiti potter Helen Cordero. Signing and telling stories has long been a method of educating children in the intricacies of the Pueblo culture.

At the Indian Market held annually in August in Santa Fe, hundreds of Native American artists gather from throughout the Southwest to sell their jewelry, textiles, and especially their pottery, from booths placed around the Plaza. Priced at just a few dollars fifty years ago, the best of Pueblo pottery can now command figures in the hundreds—sometimes the thousands—of dollars.

FURNITURE

The early Spanish settlers had few items of furniture, and these were usually the minimal practical pieces needed in everyday living. The most common item found in the colonial home was the chest, probably beginning with the giant six-board chests used to haul cargo along the Camino Real. Later, imported chests of painted leather came from China, and intricate woven and pierced leather chests were brought from Mexico.

After chests the most typical type of furniture was the bench. Highly sought after today, these early benches graced a few homes and were also found in churches. Chairs were rare in the earliest home, but as the colonists became more affluent, their need for more elegant furnishings grew. From the solid straight chairs with wooden seats, reminiscent of Spanish medieval- and renaissance-style furniture, evolved lighter chair types with Empire-period lines. Often mistaken for a bench is a small kind of table called a *tarima*, which had many uses. Other kinds of tables, both round and square, had delicate chip carving or turned spindle legs.

Collectors prize these handmade early pieces, rare at the time they were made and even scarcer today.

In the nineteenth century, young brides received fanciful painted chests from Michoacán, Mexico. New Mexican carpenters created large solid relief-carved chests and elaborately carved chests on legs; big grain chests sat under protected *portales*; and the mission fathers kept their precious vestments and silver in special long, large chests on legs. Today old grain chests hold garden supplies and firewood; and painted chests serve as cocktail, entry hall, and end tables.

There were few beds in colonial New Mexico, but during the territorial period a wide variety of bed styles appeared. Fanciful cut-outs are typical of this period.

Applied moldings and fancy work were added to doors, as well as to chests like this one.

Chests were used for the storage of valuables and were passed from one generation to the other.

The cut-out work on the apron and stretcher of this early table is atypical but appealing.

Colonial furniture is remarkable for its grace and beauty. Benches now found in hallways and on *portales* were once used in churches or as special seating in the home.

This chest-on-legs with its chip-carved design is believed to be of a type that originated in Taos in the eighteenth century. A part of the New Mexican display at the American Index Antique Show held in September 1938.

A LIGHT TOUCH

The inherent sculptural qualities of adobe and the intense light of the Southwest characterize many contemporary homes in Santa Fe, but few old adobes have bridged the gap from dark fortresses to the sun-bathed openness of structures of today. The owners of this old home have managed to let in the light without detracting from the classic features of the house. Large windows at one end are matched by a geranium-filled greenhouse at the other. Only the old ceilings of darkened *vigas* have been left in the shade.

The home is also brightened by a sense of humor in the selection of décor. An old carousel rests in the fields before the house, and the living room features a "Cadillac" couch.

White-painted floors and walls, and seven doors and windows, fill the living room with direct and reflected light. The contemporary-looking room betrays its true age in the old beams of the ceiling. At the right the unusual secretary desk was made locally in the nineteenth century.

Adam and Eve in cut and painted tin by a Santa Fe artist. A sense of humor about décor is the uniting theme of the house's furnishings and ornaments.

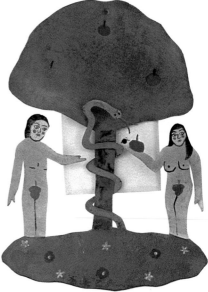

An eye chart on the glass-front commercial refrigerator challenges guests to test their vision by guessing which foods inside are real and which are look-alike plastic.

A window shutter from Africa seems at home in a Santa Fe kitchen. New Mexico shares many similarities in climate and geography with the more arid nations of Africa, and consequently has in common several cultural features, including the use of earth as the primary building material.

The unusually long kitchen table is made from an old store counter from Las Vegas, New Mexico.

Besides figures of saints and animals, folk-art woodworkers of Mexico often make replicas of churches, painted white to match the painted adobe of the originals.

A spare room is occupied by toy rabbits and dolls. Sunlight from lace curtains filters from a south-facing greenhouse.

The main bedroom also faces the greenhouse, where geraniums bloom year round.

213

TINWORK

Necessity is the mother of invention. The lack of sufficient durable and decorative materials in Hispanic New Mexico led to the creation of wonderful and fantastic works of art. When tin was brought in some quantity to New Mexico in the form of large storage containers by the United States army in the mid-nineteenth century, the local residents quickly adapted this versatile material to a variety of practical and decorative uses. Contemporary tinworkers in Santa Fe make a variety of special pieces for the Santa Fe style home—switchplates of cut and stamped tin, bathroom light fixtures made of pierced tin, and kitchen cupboard panels of punched tin.

Old designs continue to influence contemporary tinworkers.

Sconces were very popular tinware items and sometimes incorporated mirrors, which reflected additional light from the candles. Tin and glass frames were made to hold prints of the family's favorite holy image. Walls of early New Mexican homes were frequently covered with tin-framed prints and mirrors.

Painted leaves and hearts radiate
from the center of a circular sconce.

215

LANDSCAPE

When Richard Mason first saw the site for his new home, he must have felt as if he had been there many times before: the view is almost identical to that in many of his paintings—an expanse of mountains and sky in a subtle spectrum of pinks and blues, accented with pinyon pine and juniper.

Designed by Mason, the house is situated to take advantage of a scene that stretches from the Jemez Mountains to the Sangre de Cristos. Large windows at the front of the house and solar panels on the roof, which can be seen only from the road, make the house energy efficient.

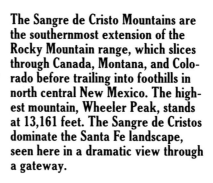

The Sangre de Cristo Mountains are the southernmost extension of the Rocky Mountain range, which slices through Canada, Montana, and Colorado before trailing into foothills in north central New Mexico. The highest mountain, Wheeler Peak, stands at 13,161 feet. The Sangre de Cristos dominate the Santa Fe landscape, seen here in a dramatic view through a gateway.

Spare and elegant, the Mason home is not without comic relief. Mason remembers calling up a friend to come to see his new Two Gray Hills Navajo rug, the dominant element of the back porch: "You could hear him thinking on the other end of the line, 'How can Mason afford a rug like that?'" His friend arrived to find that the "rug" was a nine-by-twelve trompe-l'oeil floor painting.

Large south-facing windows fill the rectangular facade, which opens onto a front patio protected by walls and hillside. Santa Fe's climate is not as mild as many first-time visitors imagine (especially shocking for those who arrive in shorts in a snowstorm in January), but an outdoor life is one of the region's primary attractions from March to October.

Simple Mexican chairs were painted in a spectrum of the artist's favorite pastels. Large south-facing windows across the front of the house open the home to both warmth and landscape.

The porch with painted Navajo rug has another optical illusion. The room is not glassed-in but open to the elements at the right. The furniture is designed to endure all seasons, and storage for cushions is built into the seating. The view from this back *portal* extends north, east, and west.

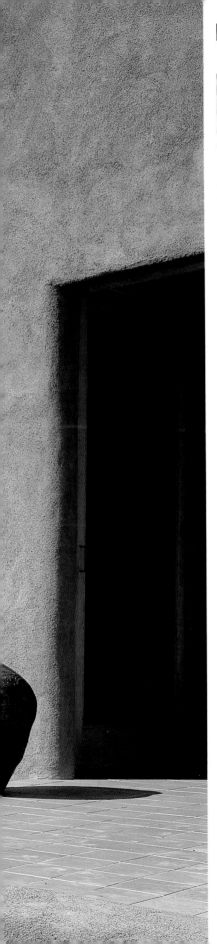

EAST MEETS WEST: CASA MATSU

Marlene and Morton Meyerson live most of the year in Dallas, but their thoughts are often with their home in Santa Fe. Built as a retreat for the Meyersons, their family, and friends, the house is designed to fill their needs for privacy, serenity, and integrity. In planning the Meyersons' passive-solar home, the architect, Robert W. Peters, took into account the Meyersons' growing interest in contemporary regional art, along with their continuing appreciation for Japanese culture. The spare lines of the Oriental landscaping suit the vast scale and elemental configurations of the New Mexican terrain.

A series of patios and clerestories sets up a rhythmic pattern against the bright blue of the New Mexican sky. The color of the sky and quality of the light in New Mexico is intensified by the lack of moisture in the air. Thunderstorms moving in over the mountains may be sudden and violent, but they usually pass quickly, leaving a well-washed landscape behind.

221

As in Santa Fe houses of the past, modern dwellings are constructed to give a view through the entire house down a hallway that passes a series of rooms. This view shows the architect's inventive use of different levels and undulating walls to create interest along the corridor. The carefully placed receding doorways give the appearance of a single opening reflected in mirrors.

Below the clerestory in the living room, a beamed ceiling recalls the *vigas* of old Santa Fe, here with the addition of light that casts an ever-shifting pattern of shadows along interior walls.

The dining room is located to take advantage of spectacular sunsets.

A BOULDER HOUSE

The architect Charles Johnson has created one of the most striking interpretations of Santa Fe style in a house in Scottsdale, Arizona. When the family of Bill Empie acquired the boulder-strewn property, they thought they might build a house that afforded a view of the monoliths scattered across the landscape.

Johnson proposed an even more startling idea: that the boulders become part of the house.

This was not the first Southwest dwelling to be sketched out on the ground, nor was it the first to incorporate indigenous rock, but it had been nearly five hundred years since the last such structure had been attempted. The so-called cave dwellers of prehistoric times adapted rock-built homes from earlier communities tucked high into caves in canyon walls. Johnson's imaginative design took this ancient idea and made it contemporary, weaving corridors and rooms through and around the rough projections of stone. Like its ancestors, the Boulder House seems a secure haven from the world beyond its walls.

Bonded to huge boulders, the house becomes part of the hilly Sonoran desert. Every view of the house presents a unique aspect, determined by the chance features of the terrain.

Interior and exterior plaster were colored to match the subtle hues of the protruding boulders.

Right: Borrowing on the concept of a shepherd's fireplace, as seen earlier in the old haciendas of New Mexico, this contemporary version has a sloping shelf above and a room-size hearth. Below: Windows are fitted in natural fissures in the rocks.

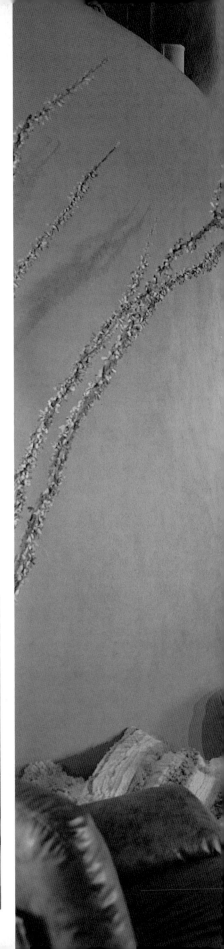

Left: Spaces open out between the rock to create living areas. In the dining room, sunlight enters through skylights fitted between the ceiling. Right: Walls spring up from the rock in this passageway that curves toward the den in the background.

A hallway through the kitchen looks toward an elegant series of *vigas* and a stairway through the rock.

TOUCHSTONE-CHACO CANYON

From about A.D. 1000 to A.D. 1300, a complex civilization flourished in Chaco Canyon, in what is now northwestern New Mexico. The Chaco culture included as many as twelve towns, each made up of multistoried "apartment" structures of masonry. The largest of these was Pueblo Bonito, estimated to have had over 800 rooms in nearly five separate levels. During its heyday, Pueblo Bonito had a population of 1,200.

The intricately planned and carefully integrated structures of the Chaco Canyon region featured living and storage rooms, interior courtyards, and the elaborate religious structures called kivas. The influence of the kiva on the vocabulary of Southwestern architecture is profound and far-reaching.

Above: Part of the curving wall of the Great Kiva is shown in the photograph at the top. The bottom photograph, of about 1920, shows the early archaeological excavation at the Great Kiva under the supervision of Dr. E. L. Hewett. Dr. Hewett stands in the foreground, his Model T parked on the level ground above.

This photograph of the Great Kiva, Chettro Kettle, was taken in about 1920. Many of these subterranean religious structures throughout the Southwest are still in use by Pueblo Indians.

Soft colors and interrelated geometric forms give this view of the house a graphic, almost two-dimensional look.

VILLAGE LIFE

From a distance the house resembles a cluster of small village homes perched in the pinyon-covered hills. Yet the building is actually an interconnected structure of separate rooms, each with an individual architectural character. The exterior walls are stuccoed in different pastel tones to emphasize their separateness.

Antoine Predock, the architect of this unusual home, saw the six units of the house as archetypal dwellings from New Mexican architectural tradition. They are reminiscent of Indian pueblos, with their interlocking multilevel communal rooms, and they are also similar to such mountain villages as Truchas, New Mexico, with their pitched roofs and staggered profiles. The source of the colors of the walls seems more Latin—Italian or Mexican—than southwestern. Invoking the "romance of the site," Predock explained that his design grew from a ceremonial approach to the use of various rooms and a desire to use the hilly terrain to its best advantage.

From a distant hillside the home takes on the look of a rural village. Each of the buildings that comprise the home has a separate function.

The bedroom gallery, one of the fragments of the composition.

Joined to the structure only at the base, the chimney tower stands guard like the village *campanile* of old.

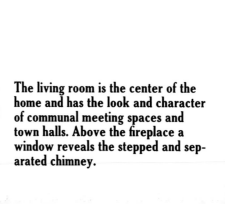

The living room is the center of the home and has the look and character of communal meeting spaces and town halls. Above the fireplace a window reveals the stepped and separated chimney.

GARDENS AND OUTDOOR LIFE

Life in Santa Fe is a celebration of simple pleasures—favorable climate, congenial company, good food, and magnificent scenery. New Mexicans live outdoors for nearly nine months a year and bring nature into the home even in winter.

Left: Nearly every vista in Santa Fe is worthy of framing. Above: A wheelbarrow serves as a movable patio garden.

Many people who live in Santa Fe today first came as visitors from other parts of the country and found it impossible to leave. The temptations of Santa Fe include a casual style of entertaining that mixes a contemporary American lifestyle with elements of New Mexican and Mexican culture. One of the favorite pastimes in Santa Fe is eating, and the cuisine of the Southwest offers a wide variety of regional dishes, many of them featuring red and green chilies, blue corn tortillas, *frijoles*, and pine nuts. Chilies, which are grown in a wide number of varieties, are more than a spice in New Mexican cooking—they are the state's preferred vegetable. Corn is second in importance, especially blue corn, an essential ingredient in *atole*, a cornmeal gruel, and in the famed blue corn tortillas. Apples are the most popular fruit, produced locally in the villages of Velarde and

Chimayo to the north of Santa Fe.

For those who make their home in Santa Fe the best time of year is often September and October—after the tourists have abandoned the streets and the guests have vacated the guest houses. As the first fires of the season are lit and the aspens turn gold in the hills, the Santa Fean revels in the special pleasures of Santa Fe.

The skull, the leitmotif of Santa Fe style and a feature made famous by the New Mexican artist Georgia O'Keeffe, and an early American rake.

OUTDOOR LIVING

Santa Fe residents' intense interest in their physical surroundings has led them to incorporate a part of nature into their homes. *Placitas*, *portales*, *zaguans*, patios, windows, skylights, and atriums bring the outdoors in and move aspects of indoor life outside. Outdoor rooms often receive as much attention to detail as those inside: walls act as windbreaks; outdoor fireplaces are installed for warmth and cooking; the ground is bricked or tiled; and the finished space is furnished with weather-resistant chairs—and sometimes the same *bancos* and *nichos* found on the interiors of adobe homes.

Because the climate is arid, with warm sunny days and cool nights throughout the year, there are no biting insects to disturb one's pleasure in the surroundings. Small indoor fountains, modest waterways, and swimming pools are often used, in the traditional Spanish and Moorish fashion, to temper the dry climate.

Top: Poolside at the home of Fred and Marion Chambers. Beyond the protective wall lies the sublime landscape of northern New Mexico. Middle: At the Pottery House, the semicircular pool mimics the curve of mountains and sky beyond. The soothing qualities of water are especially appreciated in the arid climate of Santa Fe. Bottom: When John McHugh built his home along the Camino, he made the adobes for the home at the site. Taking advantage of the resulting excavation, he added a pool to the property.

At the Camino home, the wall and raised gardens are used to create an outdoor room filled with redwood furniture and potted geraniums. Guest rooms above are reached by an outside stairway and porch.

GARDENS IN SANTA FE

The direct Southwest sun and the poor, sandy soils of the high desert make gardening in Santa Fe a bittersweet experience. As spring approaches each year, gardeners rush to begin, only to be devastated when the inevitable hailstorm strips tender seedlings, and grasshoppers and rabbits devour the remaining stalks. One method of combatting natural forces is to limit the garden's scope; another is to select native plants, which are hardy and resistant to local pests.

Plantings range from wild to sedate, from petunias to overhanging wisteria (on the far right).

Most Santa Fe homes have a walled garden or inner courtyard with a patio. Potted geraniums are often used to line the perimeter of these outdoor "rooms" and to greet the visitor at the front door. Poppies, hollyhocks, and daisies are a few of the sun-loving perennials that are found in most Santa Fe gardens. Of the native plants, *chamisa*, or rabbitbush, is most often used as a blue-green hedge that blooms yellow in the fall. Grama and buffalo grasses, difficult to raise from seed, are dependable perennials once established.

WALLS

In old Santa Fe, high walls lined both sides of narrow streets. Today adobe walls serve many uses: some shield houses from the immediacy of the street; those in the country carve a secure enclosure from the vast landscape, framing and controlling panoramic views. Walled yards with well-defined "picture windows" may also act as backdrop for gardens.

Left: The front porch of the Drum home also serves as a viewing platform. New Mexican and Mexican homes often feature a *mirador*, an elevated porch or lookout. Above: At the Boulder House, Scottsdale, Arizona, a small, walled patio overlooks the Sonoran desert.

Right: Gardens in Santa Fe run from the casual to the very informal, and building materials are often equally unpretentious. Favored materials include railroad ties and other treated woods, cedar, undressed stone, and adobe.

Abundant perennial gardens are a perfect complement to the free-spirited lifestyle of Santa Fe.

Lawns are kept to a minimum or are entirely absent. Here the wall divides wilderness from controlled garden.

The Santa Fe patio often functions as a second dining room. Outdoor fireplaces are used not only to prepare the meal, but also to provide warmth for the diners.

SANTA FE CHRISTMAS

Christmas in Santa Fe is an annual opportunity to experience the simplicity and beauty of community celebration and family ritual. You know that Christmas is on the way when you have been offered hot chocolate and its sweet accompaniment, *biscochitos*, at least four times. The crisp, cold nights fill with the scent of pinyon fires; moonlight sparkles on the snow-capped trees and rooftops. Pine boughs and red chili *ristras* hang from doors and gates. In the neighborhood of San Antonio Street, the residents begin to fill small paper bags with sand, preparing for the day when they will line their street with *farolitos*—little votive candles in the paper-bag lanterns. *Farolitos* are also put on walls and along rooftops.

Snow-covered trees and a gate captured by one of the Southwest's best-known photographers, Laura Gilpin.

Inside the Santa Fe home is the familiar evergreen tree, cut for the occasion with the permission of the Forest Service. Beside it may be a *nacimiento* from Cordova of unpainted and carved aspen or cedar. The fireplace may be decorated with black and white angels from the pueblo of Cochiti.

On Christmas eve the *farolitos* are lit, and bonfires roar in front of churches welcoming parishioners to midnight Mass. At the Indian pueblos, Mass is celebrated with dances in the church. Santa Claus comes to Santa Fe, but not with the same vehemence that he travels to the rest of the country—perhaps out of fear of being trapped in the narrow chimneys of corner fireplaces.

SOURCES

LIFESTYLE

FOOD AND TABLETOP

Chile Shop
109 East Water Street
Santa Fe, NM 87501
983–6080
The Chile Shop carries a variety of ground chili powders, blue cornmeal, *ristras*, wreaths, various harvest arrangements, chili wrapping paper. Shipping available.

The Chocolate Maven
Las Tres Gentes
418 Cerrillos Road
Santa Fe, NM 87501
984–1980
Fudge, espresso, brownies, chocolate chunk cookies, decorated cakes. Shipping available.

Chocolate Plus
125 Lincoln Avenue, Suite 113
Santa Fe, NM 87501
984–0715
Chocolates, bulk nuts, fresh fudge, large selection of truffles.

El Merendero Posa's
1248 Siler Road
Santa Fe, NM 87501
471–4766
Wholesale and retail tamales.

The Glassworks
821 Canyon Road
Santa Fe, NM 87501
988–2662
Blown glass, stoneware, pottery; open-air studio. Open May 1–Jan. 15.

Hand Maiden
102 East Water Street
Santa Fe, NM 87501
982–8368
Handmade stoneware dinnerware, utilitarian wooden items, and leather accessories.

Peter C. Handler/Finer Wines, Spirits, and Beers
518 Old Santa Fe Trail
Santa Fe, NM 87501
982–5302
Complete selection of American and imported wines, liquors, rare cordials, many exotic beers, and practical wine and bar accessories. Open six days 9:30 a.m. to 7 p.m.

House and Table
30 Sena Plaza
Santa Fe, NM 87501
982–5265
Variety of gifts for the home, many locally handcrafted items.

La Mesa of Santa Fe
225 Johnson Street
Santa Fe, NM 87501
984–1688
Earthenware dinnerware sets, pottery, glassware, linens, rugs, furniture, and accessories individually handcrafted by Southwest artists.

Lujan's Place
218 Galisteo
Santa Fe, NM 87501
983–9610
Herbs, spices, kitchenware, and Mr. Lujan's wonderful herb advice.

Nambe Mills
924 Paseo de Peralta
112 West San Francisco
Santa Fe, NM 87501
988–5528   988–3574
Nambeware sculpture, cookware, decorative art, and trophies. Shipping available.

Ohori's Coffee, Tea, and Chocolate
1215 Paseo de Peralta
Santa Fe, NM 87501
988–7026
Ohori's roasts twenty different varieties of coffee; coffee accessories, wide variety of chocolates, baked goods, and fresh teas.

Santa Fe Cookie Company
110 West San Francisco
Santa Fe, NM 87501
983–7707
Variety of cookies available for shipping in Santa Fe Cookie Company tins.

Santa Fe Seasons
1500 5th Street, No. 15
Santa Fe, NM 87501
988–1515
Gourmet food products, mustards, vinegars, jellies, spices. Available through Santa Fe fine food stores.

Señor Murphy
La Fonda Hotel 982–0461
131 East Palace 983–9243
DeVargas Mall 983–8696
Villa Linda Mall 471–8899
Santa Fe, NM 87501
Pinyon candies, chocolates, chile jellies, fudges, brittles, made in Santa Fe. Shipping available.

Madrid Earthenware Pottery
Box 300
Madrid, NM 87010
471–3450
Showroom and studio of six New Mexico potters, containing dinnerware, lamps, Mexican pottery, and planters.

Herman Valdez Fruit Stand
P.O. Box 218
Velarde, NM 87582
852–2129
Fresh fruits, red chili *ristras*, and Ramona Love Letter arrangements.

FURNITURE

Dell Woodworks
401 Rodeo Road
Santa Fe, NM 87505
988–9612
Handcrafted native pine home and office furniture. Custom designs available. Brochure and price list mailed upon request.

de Pedro International
130 West Water Street
Santa Fe, NM 87501
984–8022
Furniture, ceramics, and accessories imported from Spain. Brochure available upon request.

de Madera
Loretto Square
228 Old Santa Fe Trail
Santa Fe, NM 87501
984–8710
Traditionally designed New Mexican colonial furniture; tables, chairs, sideboards, desks, bookcases, etc.

Dooling Woodworks
525 Airport Road
Santa Fe, NM 87501
471–5956
Southwest-style handcrafted furniture for every room in the house and office.

McMillan's Woodworks
1326 Rufina Circle
Santa Fe, NM 87501
471–4934
Handcrafted furniture of Southwestern design, complete line of home furnishings, office furniture, and modular computer furniture.

Sombraje
P.O. Box 295
Dixon, NM 87527
579–4456
Custom branch-covered screens, New Mexican furniture, hand-painted fabrics, interior accessories.

Southwest Spanish Craftsman
112 West San Francisco Street
Santa Fe, NM 87501
982–1767
Spanish provincial, Spanish colonial, Southwestern, and early English handcrafted furniture and custom doors.

Taos Furniture
232 Galisteo Street
P.O. Box 2624
Santa Fe, NM 87504
988–1229
Handcrafted ponderosa pine dressers, couches, chairs, benches, *trasteros*, tables, chairs, and office furniture. Catalog and price list available upon request.

Volker de la Harpe Carved Doors and Furniture
707 Canyon Road
Santa Fe, NM 87501
983–4074
Custom furniture and carved doors at showroom and shop on Canyon Road.

SHOPS

Arius Tiles
114 Don Gaspar Avenue
P.O. Box 5497
Santa Fe, NM 87502
988–1196
Handcrafted and glazed decorative art tiles produced in the Arius studio and available in the Arius Gallery.

Artesanos Imports Co.
222 Galisteo Street
Santa Fe, NM 87501
983–5563
Talavera tile, Saltillo tile, Mexican sinks, dishes, glasses, light fixtures, and furniture. Brochure and price list upon request. Shipping available.

Colors of the Wind
345 West Manhattan Avenue
Santa Fe, NM 87501
982–8235
Specializes in windsocks, kites, banners, flags, windchimes, Soleri Bells, mobiles, and fantasyware. Custom-designed flags, interior banners, and wind sculptures for corporate, residential, and commercial environments.

Doodlet's Shop
120 Don Gaspar Avenue
Santa Fe, NM 87501
983–3771
Imports, folk art, gourmet items, antiques, handcrafted items, and unique gifts.

The Flower Market— Cash and Carry Flowers
Guadalupe at Manhattan
St. Michaels Drive and Warner
Santa Fe, NM 87501
982–9663   471–7244
Many varieties of cut flowers from around the world and a large selection of glass vases.

Foreign Traders
Galisteo and Water
Santa Fe, NM 87501
983–6441
Mexican and Spanish furniture, doors, antiques, reproductions, dishes, tile, glassware, folk art, light fixtures and rugs. Shipping available, brochure upon request.

Jackalope Pottery
2820 Cerrillos Road
Santa Fe, NM 87501
471–8539
Mexican animal pottery, furniture, clothes, dishes, and decorative items. Fountains, birdbaths, statues, clay fireplaces, and numerous gift ideas. Chili ristras and fresh chili and chili roasting in season.

Quilts to Cover Your Fantasy
110 West San Francisco Street
Santa Fe, NM 87501
983–7370
A fabric arts gallery; custom-designed Southwest, contemporary, and traditional wall hangings, quilts, and pillows. Designs by Lily and Wolf Schlien.

Susan's Christmas Shop
115 East Palace Avenue
Santa Fe, NM 87501
983–2127
Extensive collection of traditional and Southwest Christmas ornaments and decorated Easter eggs.

W. S. Dutton Rare Things
138 Sena Plaza
Santa Fe, NM 87501
982–5904
Southwest Indian pots, baskets, jewelry, and ceremonial garb.

BOOKSELLERS

Galisteo News
201 Galisteo Street
Inn on the Alameda
Eldorado Hotel
Santa Fe, NM 87501
984–1316, 984–8794, 988–2060
Newspapers, domestic and foreign magazines, books on Santa Fe and the Southwest, espresso bar.

La Fonda Newsstand
La Fonda Hotel Lobby
Santa Fe, NM 87501
988–1404
Newspapers, magazines, and Southwest books.

Los Llanos Bookstore
72 East San Francisco Street
Santa Fe, NM 87501
982–9542
General bookstore specializing in books on the Southwest, Southwest architecture, Native Americans, and New Mexico history.

Santa Fe Bookseller
203 West San Francisco Street
Santa Fe, NM 87501
983–5278
Exclusive art books, new and used, out-of-print art books and exhibition catalogs.

The Villagra Book Shop
228 Old Santa Fe Trail
Santa Fe, NM 87501
984–8884
Specializes in new and out-of-print books on the Southwest and regional greeting cards.

SERVICES

Art Handlers, Inc.
1570 Pacheco Street
Santa Fe, NM 87501
982–0228
Fine art transporting, installing, and storage.

Mr. Packer
2503 Cerrillos Road
Santa Fe, NM 87501
471–4725
Packs almost anything from everyday dishes to priceless antiques and art work. Sells packing materials as well.

Jimmy Begay
Wind River Trading
115 East San Francisco Street
Santa Fe, NM 87501
982–1592
Jewelry repair.

Laura Center
Santa Fe, NM
982–5663
Textile restoration.

Nancy Hudgins
Albuquerque, NM
292–5612
Textile restoration.

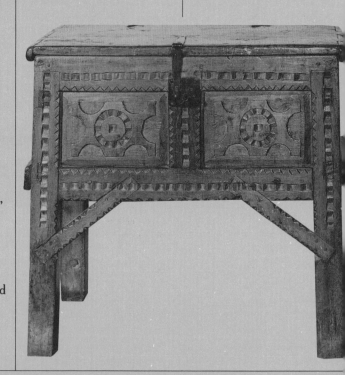

Gerald Lamb
Santa Fe, NM
984-2277
Antique furniture and pottery repair.

Richard Manifor
Whittier, CA
213-693-7432
Basket restoration.

Robert Mann
Denver, CO
303-292-2522
Navajo rug and Oriental rug cleaning.

Kathleen Morales
Santa Fe, NM
984-1625
Textile restoration.

Bob Morgan
Denver, CO
303-433-4408
Textile restoration.

Patricia Morris
Santa Fe, NM
982-3584
Restoration of artwork and documents done on paper.

One Hour Martinizing
200 East Water
Santa Fe, NM 87501
982-8606
Navajo rug cleaning, able to handle rugs up to 35 pounds.

The Persian Rug Cleaning Co.
Albert and Robert Ouzounian
2118 Temple Street
Los Angeles, CA 90026
213-413-6373
Cleaning and repairing of Navajo and Persian rugs. Expert restoration.

Neva Sullivan
Dixon, NM
505-579-4314
Basket restoration.

Sun Country Traders
123 East Water Street
Santa Fe, NM 87501
982-0467
Silver repairs, restringing, stone replacement, Indian wrap.

Robert A. Woods Construction, Inc.
302 Catron Street
Santa Fe, NM 87501
988-2413
Historic renovation and remodeling of residential and commercial buildings. Santa Fe-style construction and design.

Luis Tapia
Santa Fe, NM
471-8509
Antique furniture repair.

David Wenger
Denver, CO
303-321-4519
Textile dye analysis.

WEARABLE ART

Nancy Bloch Design
708 Canyon Road
Santa Fe, NM 87501
983-3177
High-fashion originals, handknit and handwoven sweaters, shawls, purses, and handcrafted jewelry.

Chamisa Handwoven Art-wear
221 Shelby
Santa Fe, NM 87501
982-9331
Handwoven natural-fiber women's clothing, interior design items.

Handwoven Originals
Inn at Loretto
211 Old Santa Fe Trail
Santa Fe, NM 87501
982-4118
Handwoven wearables, crafts, jewelry, interior furnishings.

The Lamb and the Ewe
211 Johnson Street
Santa Fe, NM 87501
984-8000
Handknitted sweaters and knit dressing of natural fibers.

Lewallen Jewelry
105 East Palace Avenue
Santa Fe, NM 87501
983-2657
Custom-made contemporary jewelry, original designs in gold and silver. Earcuffs and earrings designed by Ross Lewallen.

Martha of Taos
202 Paseo del Pueblo Norte
Taos, NM 87571
758-3102
Southwestern dresses, hand-pleated calico broomstick skirts, traditional Navajo dresses and shirts.

Nancy Lewis and Company
209 Galisteo Street
Santa Fe, NM 87501
988-4400
One-of-a-kind wearable art from all over the country—blouses, skirts, vests, coats, jewelry. Unusual accessories.

Origins
135 West San Francisco Street
Santa Fe, NM 87501
988-2323
Folk art to fantasy, handwoven suedes, hand beaded wear, one-of-a-kind evening bags.

Ortegas de Chimayo Weaving Shop
Galeria Plaza del Cerro
Box 325
Chimayo, NM 87522
351-4215
Handwoven vests, coats, and blankets, rugs and purses. Color brochure and order form available upon request.

Overland Sheepskin Company
215 Galisteo Street
Santa Fe, NM 87501
983-4727
Sheepskin coats, mittens, hats, boots, slippers, pelts, rugs, stuffed toys, and leather goods.

Pieces of Dreams
125 East Palace Avenue
Villa Linda Mall
Santa Fe, NM 87501
988-4668
Fiesta dresses and Western wear, custom children's furniture, Cabbage Patch doll furniture and clothing.

Plumeria
129 West San Francisco Street
Santa Fe, NM 87501
988-7412
Navajo-style velvet skirts and blouses, denim prairie skirts, Western shirts, fiesta wear, Southwestern accessories.

Rudy Ríos Boots
330 Garfield Street
Santa Fe, NM 87501
988-7150
Boots for men, women, and children. Custom boots available, handmade boots, boot repair, hats and handbags. Brochure available upon request.

Spirit of the Earth
Inn at Loretto
Santa Fe, NM 87501
988-9558
Handmade clothing and jewelry featuring lamb suedes, Laise Adzer, and an eclectic collection of ethnic and contemporary jewelry.

Styles de Santa Fe
Plaza Mercado
112 West San Francisco Street
Santa Fe, NM 87501
982-5675
Natural Southwestern style clothing and accessories.

Tierra Wools
Box 118
Los Ojos, NM 87551
588-7231
Handspun yarns and handwoven wool products in the Rio Grande tradition. Accent pillows, sweaters, rugs, table scarves, mats, and shawls. Brochure available upon request.

RESOURCES

INFORMATION

Santa Fe National Forest Information
P.O. Box 1689
1220 St. Francis Drive
Santa Fe, NM 87504
988-6940
Information and locations of camping, picnic, hiking, and areas of special interest. Camping permits are available at this location.

State Parks and Recreation
P.O. Box 1147
141 East DeVargas Street
Santa Fe, NM 87503
827-7465
Will provide information at the above location or through the mail about the facilities, schedules, and special events at the New Mexico State Parks.

New Mexico Arts Division
224 East Palace Avenue
Santa Fe, NM 87501
827-6490
This organization oversees federal grants for artists and sponsors the Artists in Residence Program.

New Mexico Economic Development and Tourism
Bataan Memorial Building
Santa Fe, NM 87503
827-6230
Provides information to people and businesses interested in relocating to New Mexico or starting a new business in New Mexico.

New Mexico State Tourism and Travel
Bataan Memorial Building
Santa Fe, NM 87503
827-6230
A division of the New Mexico Economic Development and Tourism Department. Provides information to people interested in visiting New Mexico, requests from school children, and promotes tourism.

Recursos de Santa Fe
227 East Palace Avenue
Santa Fe, NM 87501
982-9301
Recursos means resources. An independent, nonprofit center for the study of Southwestern issues past and present.

Santa Fe Chamber of Commerce
329 Montezuma
P.O. Box 1928
Santa Fe, NM 87504
983-7317
The people to ask the "who, what, where, and when" questions concerning events in Santa Fe.

Santa Fe Council for the Arts
109 Washington Avenue
Santa Fe, NM 87501
988-1878
Coordinates, promotes, and develops cultural and educational activities relating to the arts. The Council sponsors and produces programs and events year round.

Santa Fe Convention and Visitors Bureau
Sweeny Center
201 West Marcy Street
Santa Fe, NM 87501
984-6760 1-800-528-5369
Located one block from downtown Santa Fe. Accommodates 800 for banquets and 1,200 for theatre style meetings. Six additional smaller rooms.

Taos Chamber of Commerce
P.O. Drawer I
Taos, NM 87571
758-3873 1-800-732-8267
Located on the South Santa Fe Highway across from the Smith Food Store. Provides tourist information.

MUSEUMS, MONUMENTS, AND POINTS OF INTEREST

Kit Carson House
One block east of the Taos Plaza
Taos, NM 87571
758-4741

Home and museum of the famous Mountain Man, plus exhibits on prehistoric Indians and archaeology, Spanish history, and early Anglo-American culture. Registered as a National Historic Landmark.

Maxwell Museum of Anthropology
University of New Mexico
Albuquerque, NM 87131
277-4404
Anthropology museum; archaeology, ethnology, specialized Southwest collections, weaving, kachina dolls, Mimbres Pueblo pottery, American Indian basketry, musical instruments.

Lincoln County Heritage Trust
Lincoln, NM 88338
653-4372
Lincoln is a National Historic Landmark and a living community. The privately operated Lincoln County Heritage Trust owns several Lincoln properties including the Historical Center where visitors enjoy exhibits of the Apaches, Spanish, Western Black Cavalry, and the Lincoln County War. Lincoln is the site of Billy the Kid's daring escape from the second story of the Lincoln Courthouse. This beautifully preserved town is a must for those interested in the history of the West.

Museum of Fine Arts
Palace Avenue
P.O. Box 2087
Santa Fe, NM 87504
827-4455
Exhibitions feature contemporary Southwest artists and the Santa Fe and Taos masters with changing exhibitions focusing on the timely aspect of art in the

twentieth century. The museum shop carries posters, cards, books, and periodicals. Open 10 a.m. to 5 p.m. daily, April through October and closed Mondays, November through March.

Museum of International Folk Art
706 Camino Lejo
P.O. Box 2087
Santa Fe, NM 87504
827-8350
The largest institution of its kind in the world, the museum houses exhibitions of world folk art. Performances, demonstrations, and lectures continue year-round. The museum shop carries a wide selection of folk art and books. Open 10 a.m. to 5 p.m. daily April through October, and closed Mondays, November through March.

Laboratory of Anthropology
708 Camino Lejo
P.O. Box 2087
Santa Fe, NM 87504
827-8941
Designed by John Gaw Meem, it houses collections of Southwest Indian artifacts. The library and resource center are available for research. Open weekdays.

D. H. Lawrence Ranch
North of Taos
Taos, NM 87571
776-2245
Home of D. H. Lawrence. The ranch is now owned by the University of New Mexico and is often a site for weekend conferences and retreats.

Loretto Chapel
Old Santa Fe Trail
P.O. Box 396
Santa Fe, NM 87504
982-3376
Site of the miraculous staircase. Open daily 9 a.m. to 4:30 p.m. except holidays.

San Miguel Chapel—The Oldest Church
401 Old Santa Fe Trail
Santa Fe, NM 87501
983-3973
Located next to the oldest house. Open Monday-Sunday 9 a.m. to 4:30 p.m. (closed Wednesday during the winter).

The Palace of the Governors
Palace Avenue
P.O. Box 2087
Santa Fe, NM 87504
827-6474
Built in 1610, this is the oldest public building in the United States. It houses a history library, photograph archives, and various exhibitions which reflect New Mexican history and culture. The Palace gift shop carries Indian and Hispanic arts and crafts. Open 10 a.m. to 5 p.m. daily, April through October and closed Mondays, November through March.

P'O Ae Pi
185 Airport Road
Santa Fe, NM 87501
473-0435
Multicultural nonprofit gallery and gift shop specializing in traditional and contemporary art.

Millicent Rogers Museum
4 miles north of Taos on Highway 3
Taos, NM 87571
758-2462
Featuring a fine collection of Native American and Hispanic art.

Santuario de Chimayo

Chimayo, NM 87522
Thousands of believers make a pilgrimage to this lovely mountain church because of the reported healing powers of the soil inside.

Wheelwright Museum of the American Indian

Camino Lejo, (Behind the Museum of International Folk Art)
P.O. Box 5153
Santa Fe, NM 87502
982–4636
Exhibits of Southwest Indian arts and crafts housed in a uniquely shaped building. Gift shop is designed to represent a trading post. Open 10 a.m. to 5 p.m., Monday through Saturday, Sunday 1–5 p.m.(closed Mondays, October–April).

Bandelier National Monument

45 miles northwest of Santa Fe
672–4861
Large site of a prehistoric Indian ruin. Museum and gift shop, self-directed walks, camping, hiking, picnicking.

NATIVE AMERICAN CULTURE

Crownpoint Navajo Rug Auction

Crownpoint, NM 87313
A unique experience where weaver and buyer often have an opportunity to meet. The auction offers a wide selection of Indian rugs from New Mexico and Arizona. Information on dates and location are available through the Crownpoint Elementary School.

Eight Northern Pueblos Artist and Crafts Show

P.O. Box 969
San Juan Pueblo, NM 87566
852–4265
An annual craft show held for two days each July at a different Pueblo each year, featuring over 600 Indian artists. Native food and traditional Indian dances.

Indian Market

P.O. Box 1964
Santa Fe, NM 87501
983–5220
An annual event held the third weekend in August on the Santa Fe Plaza. Indian sculptors, weavers, painters, and basketmakers from all over the country set up booths for this juried show.

Indian Pueblo Cultural Center

2401 12th Street NW
Albuquerque, NM 87104
843–7270
Museum featuring art and artifacts of the Pueblos of New Mexico. Shop and Native American food restaurant. Monday–Saturday, 8:30 a.m. to 3:30 p.m.

Institute of American Indian Arts Museum

Cerrillos Road
Santa Fe, NM 87501
988–6281
Gallery representing Indian students attending the Institute from tribes throughout the United States.

Oke Oweenage Crafts Cooperative

San Juan Pueblo, NM 87566
852–2372
Handmade arts and crafts in weaving, sewing, silver, basketry, painting, pottery, and woodcarving.

Southwestern Association on Indian Affairs, Inc.

La Fonda Hotel
Santa Fe, NM 87501
983–5220
Sponsors the annual Indian Market. They also meet throughout the year to discuss various aspects of Indian culture.

EIGHT NORTHERN PUEBLOS

Cochiti Pueblo, 465–2244
Nambe Pueblo, 455–7692
Picuris Pueblo, 587–2519
San Ildefonso Pueblo, 455–2273
Santa Clara Pueblo, 753–7326
San Juan Pueblo, 852–4400
Taos Pueblo, 758–8626
Tesuque Pueblo, 988–5057

EVENTS

Fiesta de Santa Fe

P.O. Box 4516
Santa Fe, NM 87501
Four-day celebration commemorating the Spanish reconquest of New Mexico featuring parades, the burning of Zozobra, processions, music, and other festivities, held the weekend after Labor Day.

New Mexico State Fair

P.O. Box 8546
Albuquerque, NM 87108
265–1791
An annual event held in September offering a variety of exhibits, food, arts and crafts, livestock competition, and entertainment.

Rodeo de Santa Fe

Rodeo Road
P.O. Box 281
Santa Fe, NM 87504
471–4300
Three-day rodeo the second weekend in July.

Santa Fe Symphony

P.O. Box 9692
Santa Fe, NM 87504
983–3530

One of the newest organized performing groups in Santa Fe. Concerts are presented during the year at St. Francis Auditorium, beginning with a gala Labor Day weekend performance and continuing through June.

Santa Fe Chamber Music Festival

P.O. Box 853
640 Paseo de Peralta
Santa Fe, NM 87501
983–2075
In residence most of July through the middle of August performing at the St. Francis Auditorium and the Santuario de Guadalupe.

Santa Fe Opera

North of Santa Fe on the Taos Highway
P.O. Box 2408
Santa Fe, NM 87504
982–3855
Ranked as one of the top six companies in the country, this beautiful open-air theater is not to be missed. The Opera season runs from early July through late August.

Spanish Market

P.O. Box 1611
Santa Fe, NM 87504
984–6760
This market is held the end of July in front of the Palace of the Governors featuring woodcarving, *retablos*, *colcha*, embroidery, furniture, tinwork, by many well-known Spanish artists.

HISTORIC GROUPS

Historic Preservation Division Office of Cultural Affairs

228 East Palace Avenue
Santa Fe, NM 87503
827–8320
Administers the State Cultural Properties Act and the National Historic Preservation Act.

Historical Society of New Mexico
P.O. Box 5819
Santa Fe, NM 87502
983–6948
The oldest historical society west of the Mississippi; founded in 1859. The society is dedicated to the preservation of the state's tri-cultural historic patrimony and the promotion of the history of New Mexico through its annual conference, a publications program, and its own newspaper.

Historic Santa Fe Foundation
545 Canyon Road
Santa Fe, NM 87501
983–2567
The Historic Santa Fe Foundation was incorporated in 1961 to receive tax exempt donations for historic preservation purposes, to acquire and administer historic properties, to conduct research in order to determine buildings worthy of preservation, to engage in other educational activities, and to preserve and maintain the historic landmarks and structures of Santa Fe.

Old Santa Fe Association
80 East San Francisco Street
Santa Fe, NM 87501
982–1242
The Old Santa Fe Association's goals are to preserve and maintain the ancient landmarks, natural resources, historical structures, and traditions of Old Santa Fe.

Santa Fe Historic Design Review Board
City of Santa Fe, Planning Dept.
200 Lincoln Avenue
Santa Fe, NM 87501
984–6603
Review board of architectural plans of proposed building or remodeling in the designated historic districts in Santa Fe.

RECREATION
The Downs at Santa Fe
5 miles south of Santa Fe off I–25
Route 14, Box 199 RT
Santa Fe, NM 87505
471–3311
Quarterhorse and thoroughbred racing, May–September.

Santa Fe Country Club Golf Course
Airport Road
P.O. Box 211
Santa Fe, NM 87501
471–2626
18-hole public golf course, tennis, pool. Summer hours: 7 days a week, 8 a.m.–dark. Pro shop 471–0601

Santa Fe Ski Basin
1210 Luisa Suite 10
Santa Fe, NM 87501
982–4429
No overnight accommodations available at the Basin.

Taos Ski Valley
Taos Ski Valley, NM 87581
776–2295

TOURS
Cumbre and Toltec Scenic Narrow Gauge Steam Railroad
Box 789 A1
Chama, NM 87520
756–2151
A 64-mile excursion through the Rocky Mountains. Runs every day mid-June to mid-October.

Discover Santa Fe, Inc.
P.O. Box 2847
924 Paseo de Peralta
Santa Fe, NM 87504
982–4979
Guided group tours, personal tours, conventions, sales meetings, ski packages.

GrayLine Tours of Santa Fe
858 St. Michael's Drive
Santa Fe, NM 87501
471–9200
Indian Pueblo tours, city drive tour, city roadrunner tour.

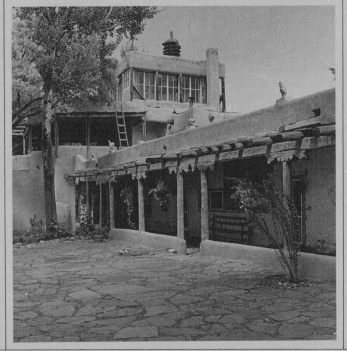

House and Garden Tours of Santa Fe
988–2811
This tour runs once a week for four or five weeks during the summer between mid-July and mid-August visiting adobe homes and gardens in Santa Fe.

J–Lor Productions
P.O. Box 1269
Las Cruces, NM 88004
523–5725
Audio tape guides available to self-tour Santa Fe, Albuquerque, and other areas in New Mexico. Map and directory included.

New Wave Rafting Company
107 Washington Avenue
Route 5, Box 302A
Santa Fe, NM 87504
455–2633
Rafting trips on the Rio Grande and the Rio Chama.

Rio Grande Rapid Transit
Box A
Pilar, NM 87571
758–9700 1–800–222–RAFT

602–998–7238 (Arizona)
Rafting trips on the Rio Grande.

Rocky Mountain Tours
102 West San Francisco Street
Santa Fe, NM 87501
984–1684 1–800–457–9223
Sightseeing tours, Indian Pueblo tours, art tours, whitewater rafting, horseback riding, walking tours, wilderness camping trips, bicycle tours, custom private tours, group services.

Santa Fe Detours
La Fonda Hotel Lobby
Santa Fe, New Mexico 87501
983–6565
River, rail, trail, and tours. Assistance with conventions, meetings, and group trips.

Sierra Outfitters and Guides
P.O. Box 2756
Taos, NM 87571
Fishing tours, cross-country ski tours, white-water rafting, river tours, horse packing. Call for information, reservations, brochure.

Southwest Safaris
P.O. Box 945
Santa Fe, NM 87504
988–4246
One day air/land adventures to the Grand Canyon, Monument Valley, Canyon de Chelly, Mesa Verde.

Wind River Balloons
P.O. Box 983
Santa Fe, NM 87504
983–8714
Hot-air balloon rides. Book 7–10 days in advance. FAA certified.

NATIVE MATERIALS

ADOBES

Adobe Bricks
P.O. Box 969
San Juan Pueblo, NM
87566
753-4846
Native products division of
the Eight Northern Pueblos.
Stabilized and semistabilized
adobes, large inventory.
Delivery available.

Eloy Montano Adobes
523 Barela Lane
Santa Fe, NM 87501
983-2172
Adobes and adobe dirt
delivered to the site. Regular
and stabilized adobes
available.

Rodriquez Brothers
Route 6 Box 27
Lower Agua Fria
Santa Fe, NM 87501
471-7570
Adobes, adobe dirt, plaster
sand. Delivery available.

BRICKS, ROCK, AND TILE

Cuyamunque Stone
Cuyamunque, 10 miles north
of Santa Fe
Route 5, Box 360 B
Santa Fe, NM 87501
455-7915
Landscaping rocks,
ornamental rock, flagstone.

Empire Block
1805 2nd Street
Santa Fe, NM 87501
982-4421
Brick, pavers, slump block,
patio products. Delivery
available.

L&P
1137 Siler Road
Santa Fe, NM 87501
471-7474
Building supplies: cement,
fireplace materials, floor
brick, glass block, metal lath,
plaster, quarry and cement
tile, railroad ties, and stucco.
Delivery available for large

quantities.

Lorenzo Ortega
142 Lorenzo Road
Santa Fe, NM 87501
983-5790
Flagstone, rock, cedar posts,
rockwalls, patios, rock
terracing; supplied and
installed.

Tiles de Santa Fe, Inc.
P.O. Box 3767
Santa Fe, NM 87501
455-7466
Handmade floor tiles for
residential and commercial
use available in several
colors, shapes, and sizes.
Write or call for brochure
and price list.

TIMBERS

**Hansen Lumber
Company and Sawmill**
West Alameda (Lumber
Yard)
1113 Calle Largo (Mailing
Address)
Santa Fe, NM 87501
471-8280   983-2774
Timbers, beams, *vigas*,
latillas, posts, split cedar,
salt cedar; lumber cut to
specifications and delivered.

Lynch Fence Company
1545 Canyon Road
Santa Fe, NM 87501
982-4076
Coyote fences supplied and
installed.

**Norton Hill Wood
Company, Inc.**
701 Airport Road
Santa Fe, NM 87501
471-2456
Timbers, beams, posts,
corbels; cut to order,
delivered.

**Rios Wood and Freight
Service**
324 Camino del Monte Sol
Santa Fe, NM 87501
982-0358
Firewood, chips, bark,
vigas, cedar posts, aspen and
pine *latillas*, split cedar,
second-hand adobes, bricks,
corbels, tiles, windows,
doors, stone.

**David Zamora
Woodworks**
2873 All Trades Road
Santa Fe, NM 87501
471-5728
Corbels cut, many different
patterns available. Custom
doors, cabinetry,
architectural millwork.

WOODWORK

**Architectural Antiques
LTD**
1125 Canyon Road
Santa Fe, NM 87501
982-0042
Antique architectural pieces,
portals, fireplace fronts,
doors, ceiling fans, windows,
corbels, ornamental ironwork,
stained glass.

Beautiful Wood
Route 6 Box 14A
Santa Fe, NM 87501
471-2140
Handmade traditional doors,
windows, and architectural
millwork. Custom design
orders welcome. Fabricators
of corian kitchen and bath
products.

Doolittle Woodcrafts
2911 San Isidro Court
(Shop)
113 Calle Don Jose (Mailing
Address)
Santa Fe, NM 87501
471-1344
Custom cabinets.

Spanish Pueblo Doors
P.O. Box 2517
2894 Trades West Rd.
Santa Fe, NM 87501
473-0464
Handcrafted Southwest-
style doors. Brochure and
price list available upon
request.

Territorial Oak
418 Montezuma
Santa Fe, NM 87501
983-5986
Traditional Southwestern
designed doors and furniture
in solid oak.

IRONWORK

**By Hammer and Hand
Architectural Ironworks**
Box 111
Rowe, NM 87562
983-7617   421-1111
(Shop)
Gates, railings, grillwork,
iron furniture, lighting
fixtures, firescreens, hearth
tools.

**DeLeon and Sons
Ornamental Iron**
East Frontage Rd.
Route 2, Box 216B
Santa Fe, NM 87505
471-8312
Custom-made fireplace
screens, gates, railings,
window bars, forged interior
hardware, latches, handles,
pulls, hinges.

**Joyce Architectural
Ironwork**
Route 10, Box 92A
Santa Fe, NM 87501
471-3971
Ornamental hand-forged
ironwork. Custom-designed
metal products of the past
and present. Historical
restoration work.

**Leonard's Ornamental
Iron**
Remuda Ridge (Shop)
137 Sereno Drive (Mailing
Address)
Santa Fe, NM 87501
471-6693
Custom interior railings,
exterior railings, gates, stairs,
spiral stairs, fireplace screens,
glass fireplace doors,
wrought-iron screen doors.

LIGHTING

Rebecca Parsons
Southwestern Light
P.O. Box 548
Santa Fe, NM 87504
473-1077   988-3419
Handmade ceramic light
fixtures available in seven
natural clay colors; ceiling-
mounted lanterns and
clusters, wagon wheel
chandeliers, wall mounts, and
table lamps. Brochure and
price list available upon
request.

**Juliana Young Clay
Lights**
P.O. Box 2638
Santa Fe, NM 87504
982-3940
Original handcrafted
stoneware light sconces, one-
of-a-kind sculptural images of
plants, animals, birds,
masks, gargoyles.

NATIVE PLANTS

Agua Fria Nursery
1409 Agua Fria
Santa Fe, NM 87501
983-4831
Southwestern trees and
shrubs, native plants, roses,
bedding plants, house plants,
garden supplies.

Plants of the Southwest
1812 2nd Street
Santa Fe, NM 87501
983–1548
Native seeds, Southwest plants, shrubs, consultation and estimating; installation available.

Santa Fe Greenhouses, Inc.
2904 Rufina Street
Santa Fe, NM 87501
473–2700
Native drought-resistant plants, organic fertilizer and pest controls, specimen cacti, pots, baskets, and plant rental.

Sweetwater Tree Farm
Route 11, Box 236
Santa Fe, NM 87501
988–3168
Many varieties of trees and shrubs acclimated to the Southwest; native landscaping and landscaping design available.

FOUNDRIES

Art Foundry
2879 All Trades Road
Santa Fe, NM 87501
471–7184
Will reproduce sculpture of any media into bronze by the lost-wax process.

Dell Weston Art Bronze Casting
1310 Siler Road
Santa Fe, NM 87501
471–2799
Bronze foundry for artists. Specializes in ceramic shell mold that allows casting without vents or sprues. Gallery and artist's studio on premises. Brochure available upon request.

Santa Fe Bronze
East Frontage Road,
Albuquerque Highway
Santa Fe, NM 87505
471–0424
All size castings up to monumental. Lost-wax process.

Shidoni Foundry, Inc.
Tesuque, NM 87574
988–8001
Foundry, art gallery, and eight-acre sculpture garden. Specializes in monumental casting. Able to fabricate large welded steel pieces. Brochure available upon request.

GALLERIES

Jeffrey Adams Antiques
555 Canyon Road
Santa Fe, NM 87501
982–1922
Spanish colonial furniture. Art and antiques of Old and New Mexico.

Adams House
228 Old Santa Fe Trail
Santa Fe, NM 87501
982–5115
Eighteenth- and early nineteenth-century American antiques.

Andrew Smith Gallery, Inc.
76 East San Francisco Street
Santa Fe, NM 87501
984–1234
Nineteenth and twentieth-century photography.

Buffalo Dancer
Plaza Real on east side of Plaza
Taos, NM 87571
758–8718

Mailing address:
P.O. Drawer C
El Prado, NM 87529
758–8718
Santa Clara black pottery, old Navajo rugs, beadwork, kachinas, Hopi and Navajo jewelry.

Christopher Webster Art Investments
54½ Lincoln Avenue
Santa Fe, NM 87501
988–2533
Primitive native art of the Americas, emphasis on ceramics and textiles. Senior member of the American Society of Appraisers. Able to procure rare items upon request. Independent dealer of Knoll International Furniture.

Claiborne Gallery
701 Canyon Road
Santa Fe, NM 87501
982–8019
Spanish colonial art, furniture, antiques.

The Contemporary Craftsman
100 West San Francisco Street
Santa Fe, NM 87501
988–1001
Features contemporary handmade original ceramics, furniture, jewelry, textiles, and works of art.

Cristof's
106 West San Francisco Street
Santa Fe, NM 87501
988–9881
Navajo rug gallery, sculpture, paintings, kachinas.

Davis Mather Folk Art Gallery
141 Lincoln Avenue
Santa Fe, NM 87501
983–1660 988–1218
New Mexican animal woodcarvings, Mexican folk art, Oaxaca Tours, appraisal services. Works by Felipe Archuleta, David Alvarez,

Alonzo Jimenez, and wooden snakes by Paul Lutonsky.

Dewey Galleries Limited
74 East San Francisco Street
Santa Fe, NM 87501
982–8632
Fine American Western art, pottery, jewelry, representational paintings and sculpture.

Dwellings Revisited
8 Bent Street
P.O. Box 470
Taos, NM 87571
758–3377
Northern New Mexico primitives, antique Mexican doors, architectural accessories.

El Rincon
Kit Carson Street
Taos, NM 87571
758–9188
The original trading post of Taos. Specializes in jewelry and museum imports.

Fenn Galleries
1075 Paseo de Peralta
Santa Fe, NM 87501
982–4631
Specializing in paintings by the Old Taos and Santa Fe artists; the Brandywine, Hudson River, and Ashcan schools; and masters of the American West. Old pottery, baskets, beadwork, jewelry and other artifacts of the American Indian. Exotics from all over the world.

The Gallery of Decorative Arts
Maurice Dixon Association
74 East San Francisco Street
Santa Fe, NM 87501
982–8632
New Mexican, Spanish colonial, and Mexican furniture and objects of the nineteenth and twentieth centuries.

The Gallery Wall
50 E. San Francisco Street
Santa Fe, NM 87501
988–4168
Exclusive representatives for Alan Houser and Dan Namingha. Galleries in Santa Fe, Scottsdale, and Phoenix.

R. C. Gorman's Navajo Gallery
Off Ledoux, southwest of the Plaza
Taos, NM 87571
758–3250
Featuring the work of R. C. Gorman.

Elaine Horwitch Gallery
129 West Palace Avenue
Santa Fe, NM 87501
988–8997
Contemporary Southwest Art.

James Reid Ltd.
112 East Palace Avenue
Santa Fe, NM 87501
988–1147
Antique and contemporary arts, featuring designs from the workshop of the gallery; specializing in belts, belt buckles, and earrings. The gallery features eight silversmiths and three leathersmiths, each providing individual designs.

The Jamison Galleries
111 East San Francisco Street
Santa Fe, NM 87501
982–3666
Traditional painting specializing in the Southwest masters.

Janus Gallery
110 Galisteo Street
Santa Fe, NM 87501
983–1590
Contemporary fine arts gallery featuring paintings, limited edition prints, photography, and sculpture.

Bob Kapoun Vintage Photograph Gallery
107 East Palace Avenue
Santa Fe, NM 87501
982–8706
Representing nineteenth- and twentieth-century Western photography.

Keats Gallery and Antiques
644 Canyon Road
Santa Fe, NM 87501
982–6686
Antique pine country furniture.

Don J. Madtson Antiques
806 Old Santa Fe Trail
Santa Fe, NM 87501
982–4102
Specializes in American, English, and Spanish furniture and decoration, primarily eighteenth and nineteenth centuries.

Ernesto Mayans Gallery
601 Canyon Road
Santa Fe, NM 87501
983–8068
American paintings, photographs, prints, and sculpture.

Linda Mcadoo Galleries
503 Canyon Road
Santa Fe, NM 87501
983–7182
American art; consultation for corporate and private collections. Appraisals by appointment.

Morning Star Gallery
513 Canyon Road
Santa Fe, NM 87501
982–8187
Nineteenth-century Plains Indian art, Western paintings.

Mudd-Carr Gallery
924 Paseo de Peralta
Santa Fe, NM 87501
982–8206
Pre-1900 Navajo weaving, Pueblo pottery, Spanish colonial art. Appraisal service.

The Munson Gallery
653 Canyon Road
Santa Fe, NM 87501
983–1657
Paintings, sculpture, and graphics by the leading contemporary artists of the Southwest.

Native American Artifacts and Antiquities
125 East Palace Avenue
Santa Fe, NM 87501
988–9600
Native American artifacts and antiquities, sculpture, pottery, jewelry, weaving, drums, baskets, and kachinas. Books on all the above items are also available.

Robert Nichols
652 Canyon Road
Santa Fe, NM 87501
982–2145
Indian art, American folk art.

O'Meara Gallery Ltd.
409 Canyon Road
P.O. Box 369
Santa Fe, NM 87504
982–2997
Nineteenth-century American art, antiques, and Indian artifacts. Appraisals.

Owings-Dewey Fine Art
74 East San Francisco Street
Santa Fe, NM 87501
982–6244
Late nineteenth-century, early twentieth-century American art with an emphasis on New Mexico Modernists, and Santa Fe and Taos schools.

Original Trading Post
201 West San Francisco Street
Santa Fe, NM 87501
984–0759
Indian jewelry, pots, rugs, baskets, old pawn jewelry.

Packard's Indian Trading Co., Inc.
61 Old Santa Fe Trail
Santa Fe, NM 87501
983–9241
Indian pottery, jewelry, rugs, drums, and moccasins.

Gerald Peters Gallery
439 Camino del Monte Sol
P.O. Box 2524
Santa Fe, NM 87504
988–8961
Works available by American, Classic Western, and Taos artists. Appraising, restoration, framing of a single work or entire collection available.

C. G. Rein Galleries
122 West San Francisco Street
Santa Fe, NM 87501
982–6226
Contemporary prints and paintings. Turn-of-the-century European painting and prints.

Tony Reyna's Shops 1 and 2
Taos, NM 87571
Kachina Lodge 2
758–2142
Taos Pueblo Lodge 1
758–3855
Southwest Indian arts and crafts at these Indian-owned and operated shops.

Santa Fe East
200 Old Santa Fe Trail
Santa Fe, NM 87501
988–3103
American art, one-of-a-kind jewelry, Native American Pueblo pottery.

Santa Fe Fine Porcelain
Route 7, Box 124 AA
Santa Fe, NM 87505
982–0479
Featuring Ward Kerr's ceramic rabbit figures. The rabbits and accessories are carefully handmade of brightly colored ceramic.

Streets of Taos
200 Canyon Road
Santa Fe, NM 87501
983–8268
Old and new Navajo jewelry and pottery. Santa Fe shirts, paintings.

SANTA FE ELSEWHERE

ARIZONA

Terry Dewald
Tucson, AZ
602–792–9545
American Indian art, specializes in baskets.

Gallery 10
7045 Third Avenue
Scottsdale, AZ 85251
602–994–0405
American Indian art.

Heard Museum
22 East Monte Vista Road
Phoenix, AZ 85004
602–252–8848
Major permanent exhibit called "Native Peoples of the Southwest." Collections of Navajo weaving, Spanish weaving, baskets, kachinas, pottery, Native American fine art.

Hubbell Trading Post
National Historic Site
P.O. Box 388
Ganado, AZ 86505
602–755–3254
Now part of the National
Park system, but still run as
a post. An excellent place to
purchase Navajo rugs and
jewelry at fair prices.
Hubbell's home is open for
tours of life as a trader in the
nineteenth-century West.

**Native American
Cooperative**
Box 301
San Carlos
Apache Reservation
San Carlos, AZ 85550
602–475–2279
An American Indian co-
operative. Over 2,000 artists
from over 100 tribes
throughout the United States
and Canada.

Pueblo One
Richard and Charles Cleland
3815 North Brown Avenue
Scottsdale, AZ 85251
602–946–7271
Indian and Spanish colonial
art.

CALIFORNIA

**Don Bennet and Kim
Martindale**
P.O. Box 283
Agoura, CA 91301
818–991–5596
Antique American Indian
art; art shows and sales.

Kathy Whitaker Bennett
P.O. Box 1375
Blue Jay, CA 92317
213–254–1218
American Indian art.

Benson L. Lanford
Los Angeles, CA
213–850–6135
818–352–4602
American Indian art. By
appointment.

Ron G. Munn
Whispering Pines Gallery
8243 La Mesa Boulevard.
La Mesa, CA 92041
714–460–3096
Indian, Western art;
auctions.

**The Native American
Art Gallery**
215 Windward Avenue
Venice, CA 90291
American Indian art.

Southwest Museum
234 Museum Drive
Los Angeles, CA 90065
213–221–2163
Native American art and
artifacts of the peoples of the
Southwest, Plains,
Northwest, and California.

Leon Taylor
4787 North Blackstone
Fresno, CA 93726
209–224–8312
Fine Indian baskets.

Bud and Joan Towne
72056 Palm Haven
Rancho Mirage, CA 92270
619–340–6228
Contemporary American
Indian art.

COLORADO

Denver Art Museum
100 West 14th Avenue
Parkway
Denver, CO 80204
303–575–2793
Native American costumes,
baskets, weaving, pottery,
jewelry.

Jay Evetts
Yoder, CO 80864
303–478–2248
American Indian art.

Mark Winter
P.O. Box 1096
Pagosa Springs, CO 81147
303–264–5957
Navajo blankets.

FLORIDA

Four Winds Gallery
1167 3rd Street South
The Corner Building
Olde Naples, Florida 33940
Native American pottery,
textiles, and jewelry.

ILLINOIS

Field Museum
Roosevelt Road and Lake
Shore Drive
Chicago, IL 60605
312–922–9410
Collections of American
Indian artifacts and life-size
exhibits of American Indian
lifestyle.

**George and Grace
Marsik**
Northbrook, IL 60062
312–564–1023
North American Indian art,
classic Navajo blankets, and
historic pottery. By
appointment.

**The Medicine Wheel
Gallery**
2234 North Fremont
Chicago, IL 60614
312–871–4467
North American Indian art.

NEW YORK

Gallery 10 Inc.
29 East 73rd Street
New York, NY 10021
212–861–5533
Contemporary Indian art,
sculpture, classic Navajo
blankets, and historic
pottery.

**Eleanor Tulman
Hancock**
202 Riverside Drive
New York, NY 10025
312–866–5267
North American Indian art.
By appointment.

Alan Kessler
Box 165
Coldbrook, NY 13324
315–845–8360
Fine Plains, Eastern
Woodlands, and
Southwest Indian art.

**The Museum of the
American Indian**
Broadway and 155th Street
New York, NY 10032
212–283–2420
Permanent exhibits of the
artifacts of the Indian people
of North, Central, and South
America; pottery, jewelry,
textiles, baskets, garments,
weapons, and kachinas.

George Terasaki
10 East 67th Street
New York, NY 10021
Dealer in North American
Indian art.

Trotta-Bond
RD #4 Box 285
Pleasant Valley, NY 12569
914–677–9074
American Indian art.

PENNSYLVANIA

Fred Boschan
Lafayette Hills, PA 19444
215–825–0928
American Indian art.

TEXAS

Balene, Inc.
1310 McDuffie Street
Houston, TX 77019
713–523–2304
American Indian art.

INDEX

PHOTOGRAPH CREDITS

Numbers indicate pages. Numbers in parentheses indicate archive negative numbers.

Key: T–Top Row
      M–Middle Row
      MT–Middle Top Row
      MB–Middle Bottom Row
      B–Bottom Row
      L–Left
      C–Center
      CL–Center Left
      CR–Center Right
      R–Right

Amon Carter Museum, Photograph Archives, Laura Gilpin Collection: 123B; 142TL; 248–49.

Antiques, 161; Paul Rocheleau: 96–101.

Bennett, James P.: 25TL; 36MTL

Clark, William: 23; 25BR; 26; 36TL, TR, BCR; 54T; 66T, ML, MR; 110TC; 142TR, MR; 162; 172BL; 176–77; 203TR; 251TR; 258R; 259B.

Drum, Jim: 242T; 244.

Hoptman, David: 21BC; 25BL; 29L; 246L.

Klamm, Ed: 78–79; 236.

Mather, Christine: 16L; 21TL, MC, BR; 22B; 34; 35MBR; 36MTR, MBL, BL; 37; 92; 94; 110MC; 119L; 138R; 149R; 151ML, BR; 237; 242BR; 246TR; 247TL, BL.

Mather, Davis: 118TL, TR, B; 119TR; 120.

Moses, Forrest: 243L.

Museum of International Folk Art, Jack Parsons: 203TC (FA7734–61).

Museum of New Mexico Photograph Archives: 12 (22468–8); 40B(51927); 52T(12463); 95L(20914); 95R(1189); 102T(10518); 142BL(105951); 154B(8879); 187R(3712); 207TR(1916); 231(80822); 231TR(66944); 231BR(80818); 261B(29893); 262B(10718).

Bennett, George C.: 11(55003).

Dingee, Tyler: 122T(59486)

Goodwin, Sage H.:142ML(119540); 142BR(119528).

Hook, W. E.: 53B(117392).

Kernberger, Karl: 4(4335); 102B(29034); 103(43325, 29006).

Knee, Ernest: 122B(59509); 123T(59483); 259(59477).

McKittrick, Margaret: 9.

Nusbaum, Jesse: 66BR(16745); 186L(61635); 186BR(61486).

Parkhurst, T. Harmon: 52B(7847); 53T(43597); 102M(32106); 169BR(1859); 170(50981, 50992); 171B(13634); 174B(31126); 175B(88083); 257(4552).

Snow, Milton: 182BL(112294).

Wittick, Ben: 10(16333); 182TL(16480); 182TR(15986); 182BR(16471); 183(16304); 185L(48998).

Nohl, Mark: 35MTR, MBC, BR; 36TCL, TCR, MBR; 121; 202BR; 250; 251TL, ML, MC, MR, BR.

Parsons, Jack: 14–15; 16R; 17–18; 21TC, TL, ML, BL; 22T; 25TC, MC, MR, BC; 27B; 28; 29R; 30–33; 35TL, TR, MTL, MTC, MBL, BL, BC; 36MTCL, MTCR, MBCL, MBCR, BCL; 54B; 55B; 60–65; 68T; 70; 72TL; 75; 80–83; 86–88; 91; 110BL; 116TL, TR; 118TC; 126–29; 130B; 132–33; 136B; 140T, R; 141L, TC, TR; 144–47; 149L; 150; 153; 163–67; 168TL, BL, BC, BR; 169TL, TR, BC; 180; 181BL, BR; 184; 185; 188; 191; 198–200; 201L; 202T, BL; 203TL, BL, BR; 205TL; 208–13; 224–29; 239; 242BL; 243R; 245R; 247R; 260B; 261T.

Reck, Robert: 13; 20; 38–39; 40T; 41–51; 56–59; 67; 68BL, BR; 69; 71; 72BL, R; 73; 74; 76–77; 84–85; 89–90; 104–109; 114–15; 116B; 117; 124–25; 130T; 131; 134–35; 136T; 137; 138L; 139R; 140B; 141BR; 148; 151T, BL; 152; 154T; 155–60; 168TR; 172TL, TR, MR, ML, BR; 173, 178–79; 181T; 187L; 189; 190; 192–97; 204; 205TR, B; 216–23; 232–35; 238; 240–41; 253; 255; 256; 259B; 260T; 262T.

Satkowski, Sheila: 55T; 143.

Woods, Sharon: 21MR; 24; 25TR, ML; 27T; 35TC; 36BR; 93; 110TL, TR, ML, MR, BC, BR; 111; 201R; 251BL.